Praying Our Lives

"You don't have to be a believer to pray with this book. All you need is a longing, a thirst, an ache, even, to connect with the living God. If you have patience to enter into these words and let them awaken your slumbering soul, who knows? Perhaps you will touch God. Or, what if God, who summoned you into being, is waiting to touch you?"

Helen Prejean
Author of *Dead Man Walking*

"There are so many things to pray about. There are so many ways to pray! Sometimes we need words. Sometimes we seek ancient words. Sometimes the words spring spontaneously from the heart. Always, prayer is easier than we thought. Bernstein takes the whole matter and leads us through all the ordinary and extraordinary experiences that make up our days and that are imbedded in the seasons. As a woman of prayer, she knows how to help women pray. While much of the book is Catholic, it is also catholic and easily accessible to all women who long to live life with and in God."

Gertrud Mueller Nelson
Author of *Pocket Prayers*

"Women will find here inspiration, encouragement, and a powerful sense of solidarity with women of faith past and present, who bring to prayer common experiences and shared hopes. With creativity, wisdom, and sensitivity, Eleanor Bernstein gently invites women to pray out of their relationship with God, to become more deeply aware of the grace-filled everyday moments that are themselves prayer, and to realize their connectedness with the wider tradition and community of faith. *Praying Our Lives* is a welcomed volume for women seeking a thoughtful and accessible guide to deeper prayer."

Anne Koester
Author of *Sunday Mass*

"Eleanor Bernstein's wonderful *Praying Our Lives* will enrich and inspire your personal dialogue with the Lord. Eleanor walks alongside her reader as a trusted spiritual counselor, paving the way, pointing out new insights, and introducing us to spiritual companions who have gone before us on the path to heaven. This book will have a place in my daily quiet time and will be a new favorite gift for the special women in my life!"

Lisa M. Hendey
Author of *A Book of Saints for Catholic Moms*

"*Praying Our Lives* will indeed serve women as a treasury of prayer. Just as a woman goes to her jewelry box to find a piece of jewelry to suit an occasion, each woman will find in this book prayers for situations that are particular to her, prayers that resonate with the experience of women who have walked in the company of the Holy One. I know that I will make it available to women I accompany in spiritual direction, and I will recommend it to retreatants."

Marie Schwan, C.S.J.
Author of *Come Home*

"Along with the challenge for constant prayer, *Praying Our Lives* calls us to a deeper, more extensive life of prayer. This book invites us to recognize God in our ordinary experiences and offers prayers for those times when we find it most difficult to pray. Filled with a variety of resources, from traditional prayers to prayers from scripture and the holy men and women who have gone before us, this tool draws us closer to the One who wants to be with us in our every day and our every night."

Julie Cragon
Author of *Bless My Child*

Praying Our Lives

A Woman's Treasury of Catholic Prayer

edited by Eleanor Bernstein, C.S.J.

ave maria press notre dame, indiana

Unless otherwise indicated, scripture quotations are from the *New Revised Standard Version* Bible, copyright © 1993 and 1989 by the Division of Christian Education of the National Council of Churches of Christ in the USA. Used by permission. All rights reserved.

Founded in 1865, Ave Maria Press is a ministry of the United States Province of Holy Cross.

www.avemariapress.com

ISBN-10 1-59471-270-0 ISBN-13 978-1-59471-270-8

Cover image © Istock Images.

Cover and text design by Katherine Robinson Coleman.

Printed and bound in the United States of America.

Library of Congress Cataloging-in-Publication Data
Praying our lives : a woman's treasury of Catholic prayer / [compiled by] Eleanor Bernstein.

p. cm.

Includes bibliographical references.

ISBN-13: 978-1-59471-270-8 (pbk.)

ISBN-10: 1-59471-270-0 (pbk.)

1. Catholic women--Prayers and devotions. 2. Catholic Church--Prayers and devotions. I. Bernstein, Eleanor.

BX2170.W7P73 2011

242'.643--dc23

2011033435

green press INITIATIVE

Contents

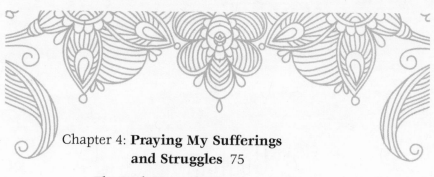

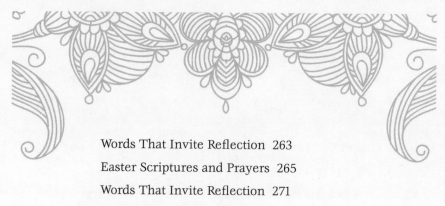

Preface

While my name appears on the cover of this book, the volume has many contributors. Beyond the published writers, however, *Praying Our Lives* would not have come to birth without the inspiration and influence of those who planted seeds of faith and taught me the ways of prayer.

I am grateful to my mother, from whom I first learned the words of prayer, kneeling with her at bedside. To my father, for his witness of a faithful, dedicated, and generous life. To Theresa, *who has prayed her life* with faith, trust and joy. To +Nonie Elliot, C.S.J., who modeled life as prayer. To sisters in faith, companions on the journey, with whom I have shared decades of praying together. To teachers and professors over the years, who provided the theological building blocks of the tradition of Christian prayer. Some of their works are included in this volume. To the many who allowed their texts to be part of this treasury.

Heartfelt appreciation to my religious Congregation of St. Joseph of Medaille, for the priceless gift of an education that opened doors—into the treasuries of literature, theology, and liturgical studies. My love for language and thirst for theological grounding were nurtured by the fine teachers whose influence marks these pages. The shortcomings are mine alone.

I am especially indebted to +Lydia Champagne, C.S.J., weaver of words, for nurturing in me a love and delight in the beauty of language and a passion for the theological quest; to Marie Schwan, C.S.J., invaluable conversation partner throughout this project; to professors Dr. William Storey, who breathed life into the Tradition; to Dr. Robert Taft, S.J., who invited me to glimpse the Mystery at the heart of liturgical prayer; to +Dr. Mark Searle, whose vision wedded liturgy and life. Their wisdom and learning provided, I trust, a firm base for this collection.

Countless others gifted me with ways of seeing, knowing and loving the life out of which authentic prayer springs. That is the ground in which *Praying Our Lives* took root.

And finally, to Robert Hamma, Editorial Director at Ave Maria Press, who saw potential in the initial draft of this manuscript, and to Patrick McGowan for patient and painstaking work to bring the manuscript to publication in the face of many challenges.

That in all things, the living God be praised!

8 September 2011

Nativity of Mary

An Invitation

"Prayer is the mortar that holds our house together," wrote Teresa of Avila in the sixteenth century. Her words resound today with a compelling truth: prayer—nurturing a relationship with God—sustains us in this daring adventure we call life.

Our Christian tradition preserves volumes of writings on the subject of prayer. Recent decades evidence a surging popular interest in prayer and spirituality, along with invaluable research focused on women's contributions. Recognizing that women's experiences throughout the history of the Church are being sought out, recovered, valued, and mined for theological and spiritual insights (some of them long overlooked), I offer this volume.

Praying Our Lives is an invitation to women to "come away and rest a while," to awaken to prayer and realize that life is always *with* God, *in* God. Prayer is about spending time in communion—at times using words—with the One who is the Source and Ground of our being: Holy Mystery, Creator, Word and Life-giving Spirit, Father and Mother, Son and Brother, Counselor and Advocate.

Praying Our Lives offers a vast selection of women's approaches to prayer—ancient and modern, traditional and contemporary. More than that, however, it offers an invitation to women to pray their own experiences, to reflect on and to *trust* their relationship and communion with the God revealed in the depths of every human heart through the life one lives. It is an invitation to recognize in ordinary experiences (and the occasional out-of-the-ordinary ones as well) *windows* that allow one to catch a glimpse of the Holy One—the Mystery we name God. These windows invite a long, loving look at the One who dwells at the heart of life, of all life, inseparable from our joys and sorrows, successes and disappointments, health and sickness, labor and leisure, confidence and fears.

Quite simply, our God is the God who lives in every human heart. That is the faith which inspires and supports all prayer. When we join our voices with the great communion of saints, with believers of all ages, our prayers rise like incense, out of our own depths, to praise the One who holds us in life. Our prayer enfolds our wounded world in a garment of mercy, compassion, and care. Can we imagine that the stirring we feel within us may indeed be the Spirit's prophetic movement urging us to name the injustice we see, to speak on behalf of the voiceless, to give word to the visions we glimpse of a better world for all God's family?

One final note—included in this volume are a few texts belonging to the wider Christian tradition and a few emerging from other religious traditions. These texts, nonetheless, reflect the authentic experiences of the human spirit open to the sacred dimension present in all of life, that Holy Mystery that draws us into relationship. These texts, notable for their simplicity and depth, are catholic—universal—in the truest sense.

Let Us Pray

Whether I look back on a lifetime of praying or whether I feel a stronger call to prayer more recently, my life story is rich with all the persons and places, events and experiences that have shaped me and brought me to be the person I am. And when I pray, I pray as who I am, unique and irreplaceable, cherished by a loving God, reflecting the blessings I've received and the burdens I carry, a fragile earthen vessel bearing the grace of God.

Prayer expresses itself in many forms. At times, I may feel drawn to one or another way of praying. This volume provides many paths to prayer, offering the reader a variety of ways to respond as the Spirit leads.

Paths to Prayer

At times prayer springs up out of an unexpected *experience*, needing no special place or text—only the occasion that calls me to an awareness of God at this moment. Personal life experience often draws prayer out of us, as we rejoice in life's joys, wrestle with life's struggles, and reach for strength beyond our own.

Prayer can burst out spontaneously; for example, as in a moment of extreme fear, I steer my skidding car on an icy road: "O, my God! Help me!" Or joyously at the first sight of a newborn: "Thank you, thank you, God, for this miracle of healthy new life!"

We all know moments like these—when something deep inside leaps up, goes beyond us. Oftentimes, there are no words; our spirit soars—and we touch the heart of God. No memorized prayers, no formulas needed—the gift of communion is bestowed. We are one with the God who is all love and compassion and mercy, the God who shares our joys and who weeps our tears. But how can we make this deeper level of existence part of each day? By learning to live contemplatively. Is this not what we are made for? The origin of the word contemplative comes from words meaning "a place for observation." As we mature, we lean into this way of living. We begin to grow in awareness of the Mystery within us and around us. We come to see, to hear, to feel more deeply from within the sacredness of our days, the holiness of all life. We long to enter this deeper level of existence that brings meaning into the hectic and harried pace of our lives. But how do we get there? Is there a road map?

Praying Our Lives offers a variety of helps along the way. It is an invitation to personal reflection and prayer in many different forms. Within the text, you will discover and rediscover diverse resources for prayer—some familiar, some refreshingly new.

Experience

Everyday life provides a continuing succession of experiences that invite us to prayer, some of unique import, some very matter-of-fact and ordinary. Whatever the event—the encounter, the disappointment, the elation—for the "awakened soul," these become pathways of access to the Mystery residing within.

As human persons with the ability to reflect on ourselves and our relationships, as well as on events in the wider community and the wider world, we know that our own life experience affords ample material for prayer. Women of faith, we believe in the Spirit alive and active within. When we do not know how to pray, Paul writes, "the Spirit groans within us." And that Spirit not only groans, but rejoices, pleads, laments, loves, comforts, supports all who are beloved of God. The ordinary happenings of our days, the extraordinary events that claim our attention, our concern, our jubilation—all these can be "the stuff" of our prayer.

In this section of *Praying Our Lives,* a wide collection of prayer texts "word" diverse human experiences and situations. Some may be familiar; others, perhaps, will awaken in you new ways of praying.

Creation

In our growing awareness of the presence of God pulsing through all of creation, how often do we stand silent before the awesome beauty that surrounds us? Wordless prayer spills out in reverence for nature's gifts; we reflect that we are a part of this great web of life.

Gerard Manley Hopkins wrote, "The world is charged with the grandeur of God." Creation, in its awesome splendor, silently invites praise and thanksgiving. In the lyrical poetry of Psalm 19,

> The heavens are telling the glory of God;
> and the firmament proclaims his handiwork.
> Day to day pours forth speech,
> and night to night declares knowledge.

God's first word to us is "creation," the universal language that belongs to all peoples of all ages. We are graced today with compelling insights into the interrelationship of all that is—seas and stars, rocks and robins, ferns and fishes, the entire family of nations that people planet Earth. So it is that nature itself invites and inspires prayer; its very being is an unending song of praise.

Centuries ago, many of the mystics recorded their visions of the beauty of God in creation. Native Americans declared the earth is, indeed, a holy place. Contemporary artists, naturalists, ecologists urge us to reverence the earth. Prayer texts, poetry, and meditative reflections in this section invite our contemplation and draw us to prayer.

Scripture

Christians often feel a call to pray the scriptures—reflectively, meditatively—entering into passages that tell a story or that speak God's loving, comforting word. Believers and disciples, we often return to our sacred story in scripture. In modern times, we have come to be more familiar with Bible reading, and, no doubt, have our own favorite stories from the gospels, passages from the writings of the apostles, or from our Jewish ancestors in the faith. You will find throughout this book a variety of scripture passages on different themes.

Within the Bible, the Book of Psalms occupies a unique place. It is the prayer book of the Bible. The psalms are the prayers that Jesus, Mary, and Joseph prayed together in their Jewish home, as they journeyed to Jerusalem, at worship in the synagogue or in the Temple. At times, we may find it difficult to resonate with the language in certain psalms; nevertheless we can recognize, on the whole, that the Book of Psalms reflects a wide range of human experience and emotion—feelings that often parallel our own.

Using the Psalms and other great prayer texts from the Bible, chapter four is made up of passages that begin with a brief introduction, followed by a short prayer, and a suggested way of concluding the prayer. To pray the scriptures means not only to read the sacred text, but also to spend a period of time in reflection: how can I connect my life experiences with the experiences of my biblical forebears? How does this passage illumine my own faith experience?

In addition to this section on using the scriptures for prayer, each section of this book contains scripture passages pertinent to the theme.

Traditions

In certain circumstances, you may be drawn to find a *prayer text*—a written prayer or reflection—that expresses what you are feeling, where your own spirit is settling at this time. Among these are prayers handed down from our mothers and sisters in the faith, those who walked before us and whose light continues to illumine our way. This volume includes many prayers from the Catholic Christian tradition. From that storehouse, we select treasures new and old—prayers to Jesus, to the Holy Spirit, to Mary, and to the saints. The familiar texts remind us, perhaps, of our earlier years. We recall the generations of believers who have walked before us, praying these same words; we are grateful for their faith.

Liturgies, Feasts, and Seasons

Our Christian heritage of rituals and symbols nurtures prayer. Its wealth of meaning speaks to believers in every age a new and life-giving word. Within the centuries-old tradition of Catholic (and Christian) worship, *the* liturgy—its symbols and silence, words and actions, feasts and seasons—also serves as a rich resource for personal prayer. Poetic reflections on key elements of the eucharistic celebration invite us to insight and appreciation of what may have become very familiar. When we reflect on and contemplate these elements of our common Christian ritual, familiar gestures, prayers, and symbols break open and reveal the Holy at the heart of our faith. Later, when we return to the community celebration, we participate with new eyes and a new heart. The communal celebration comes alive in new and meaningful ways.

Prayer at various times of the day—morning, midday, evening, and night—occupies a significant portion of this chapter. Both traditional and contemporary, the texts provide a way of turning to God, whether briefly or for a longer time, especially at the beginning and ending of the day.

The section also provides a focus for prayer during the seasons of the liturgical year: Advent, Christmastide, Lent, Eastertide, and Pentecost. Each season suggests scripture passages, prayer texts, and short reflections to enrich prayer and draw us into the mystery of Christ's life pulsing within the Church—within believers of every generation.

Words That Invite Reflection

At the end of several sections you will find brief texts selected for the additional insight and wisdom pertinent to the topic. They are not prayers addressed to God per se. They are "seeds" meant to inspire your own meditation and reflection. Throughout human history, thoughtful persons have penned their own observations about the meaning they find as they reflect on their own life experiences, the richness of faith, the value of relationships.

Hopefully, their words will serve to draw you into further reflection and meditation, leading you more deeply into your own life and its profound mystery. Perhaps you will find that another's wisdom mirrors your own; at other times, the reflection may clarify your own experience, provide a new layer of meaning. Treasure the shared wisdom handed on to us for our enrichment.

Making Time and Space for Prayer

Even though we may value and desire a life enriched by prayer, how do we develop a habit of praying? A first step begins with the simple word time. Decide to carve out of your busy day a time that is convenient and works with your schedule. Do you have ten or fifteen minutes at the start of your day? Or at the end of your day? Would something different work for you? What does your daily rhythm allow? What is do-able?

You may find the evening a prayerful time to reflect on the happenings of the day; if you are a morning person, you may prefer to begin the day with prayer before the busyness of the day takes over. Some days you may feel the need for a more extended time for prayer. Periodically, you may feel the call or need for a day or weekend of reflection or a retreat.

It's best to choose a time when you are least likely to be disturbed. You'll want to be able to stick to your plan. Once you find a good rhythm, it becomes easier to stay with it; in fact, you'll find that when something unexpected keeps you from this prayer time, you actually miss the experience.

Regarding prayer space, do you know of a quiet corner at home or a place outside where the beauty of nature invites contemplation? Could it be over your first cup of coffee in the morning? Watching the sunset at day's end? Some prepare a little table with a religious image or an icon, perhaps a candle and a colorful cloth to create a prayerful atmosphere. And, of course, a comfy chair.

Women through the Ages

Finally, because this is a prayer book for women, you will note an emphasis on prayers and writings by holy women, traditional and contemporary, from across the centuries and around the world. Prayers of biblical women, prayers of the mystics, and prayers of present-day saints invite us to address with confidence the eternal One. Their experiences can reveal us to ourselves, assuring us that the Spirit breathes within and shows us the face of God today.

Throughout this collection, you will meet great mystics who traveled before us—women like Julian of Norwich, Teresa of Avila, Hildegard of Bingen, Mechthild. While their names may seem like oddities from an ancient age, their words sound loud and clear in this twenty-first century. Their personal encounters with God convey strong conviction of how deeply they are loved and called by God to speak and write of their experiences. Texts of their prayer and meditation, as well as shorter quotations pregnant with meaning, spill over these pages.

Not only our centuries-old sisters, but modern women—such as Blessed Mother Teresa, Dorothy Day, Caryll Houselander, Edwina Gateley, to name but a few—testify to the vibrant and compelling witness of women of faith in our own times.

As it was from the beginning, so mysteriously, the Spirit of God, Sacred Presence, the Holy One, vibrantly lives within us and all around us. There is no place or time where God is not. Believers, even in the darkest times, hold to this truth. It is out of this conviction that we have the confidence to pray.

PART ONE

An Invitation to Pray

What does it mean to pray our lives? We know what it means to pray prayers (texts given us by our parents or teachers or the Church, perhaps memorized in our younger years). We know what it means to answer in unison the responses at the liturgy. We even sing our prayer at times—for example, the responsorial psalm after the first reading on Sunday.

But how do we pray our life experiences? Actually, we often do this instinctively—getting the good news that the biopsy was benign evokes a spontaneous "Thanks be to God." Like the woman in the parable who found her lost coin, we sigh a prayer of relief when we discover the misplaced envelope with the money set aside for a friend's birthday gift. We may even want to tell someone about our good fortune of finding something that was lost!

There are other life experiences, ones beyond the everyday and familiar, that also lead us into prayer, or that become our prayer. Oftentimes, as we develop habits of prayer, we find ourselves absorbed by a particular prayerful experience that continues to engage our minds and our hearts even after the time of formal prayer is done. In these moments of intense experience, we become swept up by the pulsing energy—whether that energy is joyful, or fearful, or grateful, or one of loss—and our heart desires to stay there. We wish to stay because, like catching something marvelous out of the corner of our eye, we want to know more. We want to probe God's presence in this experience. God promises to meet us in prayer, and sometimes, in our experience, it seems to be happening. God is with us.

This is the same God who spoke to Moses in the burning bush, the One who answered Moses' question, "Who are you?" with the cryptic "I am who I am." Or as some scholars explained: "As who I am I will be with you." The Judeo-Christian God is the One who will always be *with-us, Emmanuel.* In this light, all that we live in every sorrow, joy, hope, dream, every fear and failure, every relationship, every labor, pain, and frustration, the insecurity and—even the seeming insanity—all, *all* is inseparable from this holy Presence, this mystery we name God.

In praying one's life experiences, we are standing with our companion God in the experience, and feeling it in our body, mind, and heart. We seek to read God's presence there, to learn what gifts are given, what unnamed or unexpected blessing is offered, even in experiences of pain and loss.

The prayers and reflections offered here serve as a starting point, a path to lead to your own inner depths, there to encounter the sacred Presence, the holy Mystery we name God. You will find a wide range of prayer texts. Choose one that speaks to you in your present experience. These prayers will invite you to address God, to pray your concerns, and pray amidst your sufferings and struggles.

Listen to Your Life . . .

Frederick Buechner, novelist, preacher, and highly regarded professor of homiletics, looking back on his life wrote:

> If I were called upon to state in a few words the essence of everything I was trying to say both as a novelist and as a preacher, it would be something like this: Listen to your life. See it for the fathomless mystery that it is. In the boredom and pain of it no less than in the excitement and gladness: touch, taste, smell your way to the holy and hidden heart of it because in the last analysis all moments are key moments, and life itself is grace.[1]

. . . and Prayerfully Reflect

In solitary prayer, we become present to the graced life that we live—graced in its happiness and its hardships, its fears and foibles, its struggles and successes. We cherish the ordinary while we celebrate the marvelous. As we tune in to what is real, awareness deepens. We begin to experience our interconnectedness with the whole human family. Anne Morrow Lindbergh saw it this way:

> Certain springs are tapped only when we are alone. The artist knows he must be alone to create; the writer, to work out his thoughts; the musician, to compose; the saint, to pray. But women need solitude in order to find again the true essence of themselves: that firm strand which will be the indispensable center of a whole web of human relations. She must find that inner stillness.[2]

CHAPTER ONE

Addressing God

Prayers of Praise and Thanks

The prayers in this section invite conversation with God, the Holy One, whose presence at the core of my being sustains me and calls me to fuller and fuller life. The silent God within awaits my attention, my response. How has the Spirit prayed within me? How is the Spirit praying within me now?

The texts that follow include psalms, prayers of holy women from the treasury of tradition, as well as prayers from contemporaries. Choose one that speaks to your heart; then, let your heart speak. The God who has loved you from your mother's womb awaits.

Psalm 104:1-4, 24, 35

As you consider the bounty of God manifest in all creation, what stirs in you? What images from nature come to mind? What do you feel? Consider the enormous generosity of God in your own personal life—the vast sweep of God's goodness to you over the years. You may want to focus on a specific period in your life. For what are you especially grateful, especially in the past few weeks? How has God's love touched you?

> Bless the Lord, O my soul.
> O Lord my God, you are very great.
> You are clothed with honor and majesty,
> wrapped in light as with a garment.
> You stretch out the heavens like a tent,
> you set the beams of your chambers on the waters,
> you make the clouds your chariot,
> you ride on the wings of the wind,
> you make the winds your messengers,
> fire and flame your ministers.
>
> O Lord, how manifold are your works!
> In wisdom you have made them all;
> the earth is full of your creatures.
>
> Bless the Lord, O my soul.
> Praise the Lord!

Psalm 146:1–2, 5–8, 10

I pray this psalm with a grateful heart for the ways that God has fed my spirit, all through my days. What desires of mine has God satisfied? What do I desire now? Speak to God the deepest desires of your heart.

Praise the Lord!
Praise the Lord, O my soul!
I will praise the Lord as long as I live;
I will sing praises to my God all my life long.

Happy are those whose help is the God of Jacob,
whose hope is in the Lord their God,
who made heaven and earth,
the sea, and all that is in them;
who keeps faith forever;
who executes justice for the oppressed;
who gives food to the hungry.

The Lord sets the prisoners free;
the Lord opens the eyes of the blind.
The Lord lifts up those who are bowed down;
the Lord loves the righteous.

The Lord will reign forever,
your God, O Zion, for all generations.
Praise the Lord!

Psalm 139:1–2, 13–16

To delight in knowing myself as "knit together in my mother's womb"—the wondrous creation of God's loving hands! Imagine this tender image. Imagine how God loves you. Be thankful for the unique person you are, cherished by a loving God. You are God's delight.

O Lord, you have searched me and known me.
You know when I sit down and when I rise up;
you discern my thoughts from far away.

For it was you who formed my inward parts;
you knit me together in my mother's womb.
I praise you, for I am fearfully and wonderfully made.

Wonderful are your works;
that I know very well.

My frame was not hidden from you,
when I was being made in secret,
intricately woven in the depths of the earth.
Your eyes beheld my unformed substance.
In your book were written
all the days that were formed for me,
when none of them as yet existed.

Te Deum (Latin, You Are God)

This fourth-century prayer expresses the cosmic praise of God—from all creation, from all humanity, from all the angels. The "Te Deum" is frequently sung at festive liturgical gatherings of the Church. Lend your voice to this universal hymn of praise. Praise God as God.

> You are God: we praise you
> You are the Lord: we acclaim you;
> You are the eternal Father:
> All creation worships you.
> To you all angels, all the powers of heaven,
> Cherubim and Seraphim, sing in endless praise:
> Holy, holy, holy Lord, God of power and might,
> heaven and earth are full of your glory.
> The glorious company of apostles praise you.
> The noble fellowship of prophets praise you.
> The white-robed army of martyrs praise you.
> Throughout the world the holy Church
> acclaims you:
> Father, of majesty unbounded,
> your true and only Son, worthy of all worship,
> and the Holy Spirit, advocate and guide.[1]

An Everyday Thank-You

This simple prayer gives thanks for health, for family, for home. Let your memory recall the ordinary, everyday gifts so often taken for granted. Name them, or even list them in a journal or on a prayer card that you will keep to use again. Let your heart give thanks.

> I give you thanks, Lord,
> for my perfect arms
> when so many have suffered mutilation.

For my perfect eyes
when so many cannot see.
For my voice that sings
when so many are reduced to silence.
For my hands that work
when so many beg.
O wondrous Lord,
to have a home, to return to it,
when there are so many brothers and sisters
who have nowhere to go.
To smile, to dream, to love,
when so many cry,
and so many hate each other.
Above all
to have little to ask you for
and so much to thank you for.[2]

Thanks for My Life

Let your prayer be a grateful remembering—your personal litany of people, places, and events that brought joy. Give thanks for the way that God has loved you through these persons and experiences. Let your heart delight in the gracious, generous gifts of God. Remember you are God's beloved; in you, God is well pleased!

Thank you, my good God,
for life filled with friends and wonderful adventure—
sharing, caring, laughing, and crying.[3]

Gratitude for the Gift of Faith

In this prayer, I am mindful of the gift of faith, and those who shared faith with me. Recall the persons in your own life who have helped to strengthen your faith. Speak with them. Share your present struggles. Pray for the grace that you need. Give thanks.

> We thank you, God, for the saints of all ages;
> For those who in times of darkness kept
> The lamp of faith burning;
> For the great souls who saw visions of
> Larger truth and dared to declare it;
> For the multitude of quiet and gracious souls
> Whose presence has purified and sanctified the world;
> And for those known and loved by us,
> Who have passed from this earthly fellowship
> Into the fuller light of life with you.[4]

Prayers of Love and Joy

In the following short prayer texts, women mystics express their experience of God's intimate and personal love and their desire for union with God. I may not be accustomed to being in the company of such holy women. Mystics may seem to live in another realm. But God desires and loves each person deeply and passionately. As I am faithful to prayer, open to receiving God's love lavishly poured out for me, my awareness of God's presence in my life deepens. Choose one of these prayers, pray it slowly from your own depths, and know that the Holy One longs for your love also.

Union with God

> Abide in me as I abide in you. . . . I am the vine, you are the branches. Those who abide in me and I in them bear much fruit, because apart from me you can do nothing. . . . If you abide in me, and my words abide in you, ask for whatever you wish, and it will be done for you. (John 15:4–5, 7)

My Soul, God's Dwelling

Give peace to my soul;
make it Your heaven
Your beloved dwelling and Your resting place.[5]

In Yourself See Me

And should by chance you do not know
Where to find Me,
Do not go here and there;
But if you wish to find Me,
In yourself see Me.
Soul, since you are My room,
My house and dwelling,
If at any time,
Through your distracted ways
I find the door tightly closed

Outside of yourself seek Me not.
To find Me it will be

Enough only to call Me
Then quickly will I come,
And in yourself see Me.[6]

Desire for God

God, of your goodness, give me yourself for you are enough for me.
And only in you do I have everything.[7]

I Am Bound to the Trinity

Lord, heavenly Father, you are my heart.
Lord, Jesus Christ, you are my body.
Lord, Holy Spirit, you are my breath.[8]

Dancing with God

I cannot dance, Lord, unless you lead me.
If you want me to leap with abandon,
You must intone the song.
Then I shall leap into love,
From love into knowledge,
From knowledge into enjoyment,
And from enjoyment beyond all human sensations.
There I want to remain, yet want also to circle higher still.[9]

To Jesus

Jesus, my Lord,
Come to me,
Comfort me,
Console me.
Visit the hearts
In strange lands
yearning for you.
Visit the dying and those
Who have died without you.
Jesus, my Lord,
Visit also those
Who persecute you.
Lord Jesus, you are my light
In the darkness.
You are my warmth
In the cold.
You are my happiness
In sorrow.[10]

When It's Difficult to Pray

The prayers that follow give me words to pray when I find it hard to pray, when God seems distant, even silent. These are prayers for the times I want to believe, but do not feel God's presence. Be assured that others have also experienced these difficulties, as these prayers express. Pray for faith, for trust that the Spirit prays within you, often with sighs too deep for words. Be gently attentive to the Spirit within.

Silent God

Even without the good feelings and the sense of God's presence, these words declare a faith, a desire to believe the silent God "who stands by me."

This is my prayer—
That, though I may not see,
I be aware
Of the Silent God
Who stands by me.
That, though I may not feel,
I be aware
Of the Mighty Love
Which doggedly follows me.
That, though I may not respond,
I be aware
That God—my Silent, Mighty God,
Waits each day.
Quietly, hopefully, persistently,
Waits each day
And through each night
For me,
For me—alone.[11]

With You

Pray this prayer slowly, reverently. Let your faith and trust be renewed as you turn to your God.

In me there is darkness,
But with you there is light;
I am lonely, but you do not leave me;
I am feeble in heart, but with you there is help;
I am restless, but with you there is peace.[12]

Prayer When I Feel My Weakness

When I feel my weakness, I pray that Jesus will give me the grace to experience his presence, and trust that he will be with me.

O Christ Jesus,
when all is darkness
and we feel our weakness and helplessness,
give us the sense of your presence,
your love and strength.
Help us to have perfect trust in your protecting love
and strengthening power, so that nothing may
frighten or worry us,
for living close to you, we shall see your hand,
your purpose, and your will in all things.[13]

A Prayer to Be Attentive to the Suffering Christ in Our Time

At times, the sufferings of the world weigh me down. What images from recent news cry out for compassion? Hold these up to the compassionate heart of God. Let your own heart reach out in love to these persons or situations. Pray that the eyes of your heart may be opened, that the ears of your heart be attentive to the cries of your suffering sisters and brothers.

Grant us, O God, we pray,
the gift of prophets and preachers in our own time,
martyrs and those who confess your name,
poets and mystics who see you,
and recognize your hand in the pages of our history.
Give us ears to hear,
hearts attuned to your action among us—
that we may recognize you crucified again,
that we may hear the voice of your prophets
and with compassionate hearts hasten our steps
to bind up your wounds.
Spirit of Love, guide us. Amen.

To Pray Truthfully

This prayer expresses an unshakeable faith that despite the hardships that come into my life, my trust is firm in the loving God who will never abandon me.

Teach us, Lord, to pray truthfully in your name.
Free us from our foolish trust in ourselves
    and in the works of our hands and minds.
Help us to pray in absolute trust
    that whatever you send us is for our good;
and help us to accept the surprising things
    for which we have not prayed.

Give us the trust that all events,
 even suffering and death,
are for us occasions to glorify you
 and, with you, the One who sent you. Amen.[14]

Lead, Kindly Light

At times, it seems that the only thing on which I can depend is faith. In the darkness, I pray to see only one step ahead.

Lead, kindly Light,
Amid the circling gloom.
Lead Thou me on,
The night is dark and I am far from home,
Lead Thou me on,
Keep thou my feet; I do not ask to see
The distant scene; one step's enough for me.[15]

Words That Invite Reflection

The texts that end this chapter are meant to invite further personal reflection and prayer. The wisdom of other believers who probe the meaning of life and its challenges can become a doorway into deeper understanding and appreciation of the life we live. In prayer and reflection, the Spirit leads us to become more aware and conscious of the Mystery that stands at the heart of all that is.

Fall in Love

Nothing is more practical than finding God,
that is, than falling in love in a quite absolute, final
way.

What you are in love with, what seizes your imagination,
will affect everything.

It will decide what will get you out of the bed in the morning,
what you do with your evenings, how you spend your weekends,
what you read, who you know, what breaks your heart,
what amazes you with joy and gratitude.

Fall in love, stay in love,
and it will decide everything.[16]

Our Lord is most glad and joyful because of our prayer. . . . Pray wholeheartedly, though you may feel nothing, though you may see nothing, yes, though you think that you could not, for in dryness and in barrenness, in sickness and in weakness, then is your prayer most pleasing to me, though you think it almost tasteless to you. And so is all your living prayer in my sight.[17]

And so Our good Lord answered to all the questions and doubts which I could raise, saying most comfortingly in this fashion: I will make all things well, I shall make all things well, I may make all things well and I can make all things well; and you will see that yourself, that all things will be well.[18]

If the only prayer you ever say in your whole life is "thank you," that would suffice.[19]

We pray the way we can . . . not the way we can't.[20]

This is the understanding, as simply as I can say it, of these blessed words: See how I loved you. Our Lord revealed this to make us glad and joyful.[21]

CHAPTER TWO

Contemplating God's Presence in Creation

"Earth's crammed with heaven," mused the poet Elizabeth Barrett Browning, reflecting on God's presence in all of creation. The unique unfolding of the seasons, an awesome starry night, the peacefulness of a sunset at the end of day, a slowly rising sun brilliant in the eastern sky, exquisite flora and unique fauna—such beauty draws us into the mystery all about us. A leisurely walk, quietly relishing the simple beauty of your garden, appreciating a nearby park, looking out your kitchen window at the darting crimson of a cardinal in flight—the list is endless. Browning's words are timeless:

Earth's crammed with heaven,
And every common bush afire with God;
But only he who sees takes off his shoes . . .[1]

Prayers for Creation

In the following texts, poets, writers, visionaries, and believers from across centuries and across cultures share their experience of God's omnipresence. Let their words be an invitation and a path to your own contemplation. Savor, relish, delight in the goodness that comes from the Creator's hand.

The Canticle of Brother Sun and Sister Moon

In this familiar text, we are caught up in St. Francis's exuberant spirit of loving praise for his Creator and profound respect for the goodness and beauty of the created world. Starting with Brother Sun, all creatures reflect the bounteous goodness and love of God.

Most high, almighty, good Lord!
All praise, glory, honor and exaltation are yours!
To you alone do they belong,
and no mere mortal dares pronounce your Name.

Praise to you, O Lord our God, for all creatures:
first, for our dear Brother Sun,
who gives us the day
and illumines us with his light;
fair is he, in splendor radiant,
bearing your very likeness, O Lord.

For our Sister Moon,
and for the bright, shining stars:
We praise you, O Lord.

For our Brother Wind,
for fair and stormy seasons
and all heaven's varied moods,
by which you nourish all that you have made:
We praise you, O Lord.

For our Sister Water,
so useful, lowly, precious and pure:
We praise you, O Lord.

For our Brother Fire,
who brightens up our darkest nights:
beautiful is he and eager,
invincible and keen:
We praise you, O Lord.

For our Mother Earth,
who sustains and feeds us,
producing fair fruits, many-colored flowers and herbs:
We praise you, O Lord.

For those who forgive one another for love of you,
and who patiently bear sickness and other trials.
—Happy are they who peacefully endure;
you will crown them, O Most High!—
We praise you, O Lord.

For our Sister Death, the inescapable fact of life
—Woe to those who die in mortal sin!
Happy those she finds doing your will!
From the Second Death they stand immune—:
We praise you, O Lord.

All creatures,
praise and glorify my Lord
and give him thanks and serve him in great humility.
WE PRAISE YOU, O LORD.[2]

The Beauty and Wonder of All Creation: Genesis 1:1–31

In the classic creation story from the first book of the Bible, we contemplate the pristine beauty of nature called into being by the dynamic Word of God. This poetic narrative invites wonder and awe at the breathtaking sweep of the whole cosmos.

Open your Bible and read the above passage from Genesis slowly, and outdoors, if possible. Or, find an indoor spot with a view of the outdoors. Let your mind's eye, your imagination, dwell on elements of creation that most delight your eyes, your ears, your senses—give thanks to the Maker of all that is.

A Prayer for the Healing of the Earth

In this prayer, we acknowledge the ways in which human carelessness has diminished the health and beauty of Earth.

We pray to see clearly and to act wisely to restore and replenish our home, planet Earth.

Great Spirit, whose dry lands thirst, help us to find
the way to refresh your lands.
We pray for your power to refresh your lands.

Great Spirit, whose waters are choked with debris and
pollution, help us to find the way to cleanse your
waters.
We pray for your knowledge to find the way to
cleanse the waters.

Great Spirit, whose beautiful earth grows ugly with
misuse, help us to find the way to restore beauty to
your handiwork.
We pray for the strength to restore the beauty of
your handiwork.

Great Spirit, whose creatures are being destroyed,
help us to find a way to replenish them.
We pray for your power to replenish the earth.

Great Spirit, whose gifts to us are being lost in
selfishness and corruption, help us to find the
way
to restore our humanity.
We pray for your wisdom to find the way to
restore our humanity.[3]

A Prayer for Awareness and Transformation

Aware of our darkness, we pray to be transformed as individuals and as members of one human family. We pray for healing, for reverence, for generosity.

Here we are, God—a planet at prayer. Attune our spirits
that we may hear your harmonies and bow before your creative power
that we may face our violent discords and join with your Energy
to make heard in every heart your hymn of peace.
Here we are, God—a militarized planet. Transform our fears
that we may transform our war fields into wheat fields,
arms into handshakes, missiles into messengers of peace.

Here we are, God—a polluted planet. Purify our vision that
we may perceive ways to purify our beloved lands,
cleanse our precious waters, de-smog our life-giving air.

Here we are, God—an exploited planet. Heal our heart, that
we may respect our resources, hold priceless our people, and
provide our starving children an abundance of daily bread.[4]

Psalm of Welcoming

The dawning of springtime, the awakening of life on Earth reminds me of the new life we celebrate in Jesus, rising Sun. I pray for a keen sensitivity to open my eyes, my ears, all my senses to Creation's coming alive again.

Sacred Parent, creator of the sun which makes the seasons
  I rejoice in the gift of ever growing light
  as the earth daily leans closer to our daystar.
With joyfulness I greet this new season of spring
  that rises from the gray death chamber of winter.
As my ancestors of old
  lit feasting fires to banish the darkness
  and to call forth the fire of the sun,
  may I enkindle in my heart
  the flames of hope in new life.
Hope rides on the springtime air,
  carried aloft upon the wind,
  filling field and forest, city and town,
  with the incense of excitement.

With awe-filled joy
  I sing of the sun, mysterious daystar
  That warms and feeds our planet
  With energy and light.
I sing with joy that your son, the sun
  has signaled once again
  the beginning of a new season of life.

Great and generous are you, my God,
    who has given us the rich variety
    of ever-changing seasons.[5]

Autumn Psalm of Contentment

The season of autumn itself is an invitation to contentment and gratitude. The overwhelming abundance of God's gifts evokes delight and joy in the sensitive heart.

O sacred season of Autumn, be my teacher,
    for I wish to learn the virtue of contentment.
As I gaze upon your full-colored beauty,
    I sense all about you
    an at-homeness with your amber riches.

You are the season of retirement,
    of full barns and harvested fields.
The cycle of growth has ceased,
    and the busy work of giving life
    is now completed.
I sense in you no regrets:
    you've lived a full life.
I live in a society that is ever-restless,
    always eager for more mountains to climb,
    seeking happiness through more and more
    possessions.
As a child of my culture,
    I am seldom truly at peace with what I have.
Teach me to take stock of what I have given and
received;

may I know that it's enough,
that my striving can cease
in the abundance of God's grace.
May I know the contentment
that allows the totality of my energies
to come to full flower.
May I know that like you I am rich beyond measure.

As you, O Autumn, take pleasure in your great bounty,
let me also take delight
in the abundance of the simple things in life
which are the true source of joy.
With the golden glow of peaceful contentment
may I truly appreciate this autumn day.[6]

A Native American Prayer

With keen sensitivity, the Native American culture reads God and God's lessons in all of creation. What word is Nature speaking to me today?

O great Spirit,
Whose voice I hear in the winds,
And whose breath gives life to all the world,
hear me! I am small and weak.
I need your strength and wisdom.

Let me walk in beauty, and make my eyes
ever behold the red and purple sunset.

Make my hands respect the things you have made
and my ears sharp to hear your voice.
Make me wise so that I may understand
the things you have taught my people.
Let me learn the lessons you have hidden
in every leaf and rock.
I seek strength, not to be greater than my brother,
but to fight my greatest enemy—myself.

Make me always ready to come to you
with clean hands and straight eyes.

So when life fades, as the fading sunset,
my spirit may come to you without shame.[7]

Great Spirit, Give Us Hearts . . .

I pray for a greater awareness of the consequences of my lifestyle, of how I often use up Earth's resources, with little concern for the needs of others, for the preservation of the goods of Earth so that future generations will have what they need. I ask the Creator God for sensitivity, gratitude, wisdom that the way I live may show respect for Earth and for all who share this planet.

Great Spirit,
give us hearts to understand,
never to take
from creation's beauty more than we give,
never to destroy wantonly for the furtherance of
greed,

never to deny to give our hands to the building of
earth's beauty,
never to take from her what we cannot use.
Give us hearts to understand that to destroy earth's
music is to create confusion,
that to wreck her appearance is to blind us to beauty
that to callously pollute her fragrance is to make a
house of stench,
that as we care for her she will care of us. Amen.[8]

Words That Invite Reflection

In our own lifetime, we see a new awareness emerging and growing throughout world communities—an awareness, concern, and reverence for planet Earth. We confess our responsibility for the pollution of air, water, soil, the overuse of Earth's resources, the extinction of numerous species of plant and animal life. Some speak of a planet in peril. As we come to see more clearly the interconnectedness of all life and all Earth's resources, we find ourselves called to enter into a new relationship with Earth, called to reverence the gift of Creation and to walk lightly upon this Earth.

"Christ laid hold of the world . . ."

Christ laid hold of the world with His human hands;
He took it to His human heart; with his body He wed
Himself to it. Our life is the response of the bride.
"Lift up your hearts."
"We have lifted them up unto God."
We have thought about the simplicity of the things

Christ chose to use, but the simplest of all and the first essential was the humanity of Mary of Nazareth, in whose flesh the Word was made flesh.
The marriage feast of the parable is here and now; and everyone has a wedding garment if he will only accept it and put it on.
Christ has laid His Humanity upon us. A seamless garment, woven by a woman, single and complete, colored like the lilies of the field, passing the glory of Solomon, but simple as the wild flowers. A wedding garment worn to the shape of His body, warm with His life.[9]

A Mystic's Vision of Earth

The earth is at the same time
mother,
she is mother of all that is natural,
mother of all that is human,
She is the mother of all,
for contained in her
are the seeds of all.

The earth of humankind
contains all moistness,
all verdancy,
all germinating power.
It is in so many ways
fruitful.
All creation comes from it.

Yet it forms not only the basic
raw material for humankind,
but also the substance
of the incarnation
of God's son.[10]

We Have Forgotten Who We Are

We have forgotten who we are
We have alienated ourselves from the unfolding of the cosmos
We have become estranged from the movements of the earth
We have turned our backs on the cycles of life.

We have forgotten who we are.

We have sought only our own security
We have exploited simply for our own ends
we have distorted our knowledge
We have abused our power.

We have forgotten who we are.

Now the land is barren
And the waters are poisoned
And the air is polluted.

We have forgotten who we are.
Now the forests are dying
And the creatures are disappearing

And humans are despairing.
We have forgotten who we are.
We ask forgiveness
We ask for the gift of remembering
We ask for the strength to change.

We have forgotten who we are.[11]

From Anne Frank's Diary

"From my favorite spot on the floor I look up at the blue sky and the bare chestnut tree, on whose branches little raindrops shine, appearing like silver, and at the seagulls and other birds as they glide on the wind," she wrote on Wednesday, February 23, 1944. Elsewhere she states, "The best remedy for those who are afraid, lonely, or unhappy is to go outside, somewhere where they can be quiet, alone with the heavens, nature, and God. Because only then does one feel that all is as it should be and that God wishes to see people happy, amidst the simple beauty of nature. As long as this exists, and it certainly always will, I know that then there will always be comfort for every sorrow, whatever the circumstances may be. I firmly believe that nature brings solace in all troubles."[12]

The Larger View

To see the earth as it truly is, small and blue in that eternal silence where it floats, is to see riders on the earth together, brothers on that bright loveliness in the eternal cold—brothers who know now they are truly brothers.[13]

The world is the abode of God, and God truly lives in the world.[14]

The high, the low, all of creation God gives to humankind to use. If this privilege is misused, God's Justice permits creation to punish humanity.[15]

With all the arguments, pro and con, for going to the moon, no one suggested that we should do it to look at Earth. But that may, in fact, have been the most important reason of all.[16]

Some people, in order to discover God, read books. But there is a great book: the very appearance of created things. Look above you! Look below you! Note it. Read it.[17]

CHAPTER THREE

Praying My Concerns

Imagine this chapter as a treasure chest with prayers and reflections on the "energy" of the heart's desire to love. In some of our most fervent prayers, we focus on the needs of those we love—spouse and children, family members, and friends. Often our minds are filled with concerns for their well-being, health, and happiness. We entrust them to God who holds them in tender love and compassion.

For Those I Love

A Prayer for Families

Take a few moments to be in touch with the greatest gift—God's Spirit within, shaping you to be who you are. In the ordinary moments of your day, how is God's gift present? What gives you strength? Hope? Joy? These are the special gifts tagged with your name on them. Give thanks!

Bless, O Lord, the families! Amen.
    Bless, O Lord, my family!

May husband and wife have the strength to love without measure.
    May they not go to bed without seeking pardon.

May infants know the gift of love
and the family celebrate the miracle of kisses and of bread.
May husband and wife on their knees contemplate their children.
May they find in those children the strength to continue.
May the brightest star in the heavens
be the star of hope for peace and the certainty of loving.[1]

A Marriage Blessing (from Nicaragua)

Pray this text slowly, reverently, as you draw close to the celebration of marriage for ones whom you love (or perhaps your own marriage). As Jesus, Mary, and the disciples entered into the wedding rituals at Cana, so should you let this occasion in your life be a time for delight and joy. Let your heart rejoice!

May God by whose will the world
and all creation have their being,
and who wills the life of all—
May Christ, the true bridegroom,
seal your marriage in the truth of his love.
As he finds joy in his Church,
so may you find happiness in one another;
that your union may abound in love
and your coming together in purity.
May his angel guide you,
may his peace reign between you,
that in all things
you may be guarded and guided,
so that you may give thanks to the God
who will bless you,
the Son who will rejoice in you,
and the Spirit who will protect you
now and forever, world without end.[2]

A Marriage Blessing from the Orthodox Church

The text of this marriage blessing invites me to consider the long sweep of years, and the life journey the new couple will make together. This vision builds on the solid rock of faith and trust that God will always be a companion on the journey.

May almighty God, with his Word of blessing,
unite your hearts in the never-ending bond of pure love.

May your children bring you happiness,
and may your generous love for them
be returned to you,
many times over.
May the peace of Christ live always
in your hearts and in your home.
May you have true friends to stand by you,
both in joy and in sorrow.
May you be ready and willing to help and comfort all who come to you in need.
And may the blessings promised to the compassionate
be yours in abundance.
May you find happiness and satisfaction in your work.
May daily problems never cause you undue anxiety,
nor the desire for earthly possessions
dominate your lives.
But may your heart's first desire be always
the good things waiting for you in the life of heaven.

May the Lord bless you with many happy years together,
so that you may enjoy the rewards of a good life.
And after you have served him loyally
in his kingdom on earth,
may he welcome you to his eternal kingdom in heaven.[3]

A Mother's Prayer

Take time to reflect on your experience of being a mother. When and how has your being a mother reflected to your family the goodness and love of God? If you are aware of times when you failed in this role, ask God's pardon and strength. Hear God speak to you . . . affirm you . . . encourage you . . . thank you for the gift of yourself. Hear God's delight that you have been co-creator of new life, and that you continue to nurture new life.

> Loving God, you are both Father and Mother to us.
> You gave us your own Beloved Child Jesus
> that we may come to see, from his words and deeds of compassion
> how much you care for us.
> You gave us Mary, our Mother,
> faithful disciple, who treasured your word in her heart.
> Like her, may I be ever attentive to your word.
> Make me sensitive to the needs of my children
> that they, like Jesus, may grow in wisdom, age and grace.
> May they be joyous in their living,
> compassionate in their loving,
> and generous always in your service.
> In Jesus' name, I pray.

A Stepmother's Prayer

The vocation of a stepmother brings its own unique needs and challenges. This prayer names many of those situations.

Use the prayer to ponder and reflect upon your own experience and let it guide you in naming your own struggles, your joys, what helps you, and what makes your heart sing.

God of my life, you have called me into a holy and at times fearsome journey of being a stepmother.

I pray:
When I am bewildered before the awesome task of building a communion
of what has been separate and distinct,
help me to remember that You are the Center of our lives.

When momentarily I forget the love that first called us into this marriage,
please, bring me back to the precious memory of its beginning.

When it feels as if my efforts are taken for granted,
bring me to an awareness that stepmothering is a holy vocation
and a call to follow Jesus.

When our children play one against the other,
help my husband and me to hold each other tenderly.

When I am tempted to regret what I gave up
to enter into this marriage
give me an awareness of the many gifts that come to
me each day
through each member of this family.

When others expect me to do things differently than I have been accustomed to,
give me, O God, a generous and creative heart.

When I am aware of the losses that our children have endured—
the loss of a mother, of a home, of space, of ways of doing things
that shaped their earlier lives—
fill me with a deep compassion that is healing.

When I am most in touch with the goodness, the sweetness, the giftedness
of our children,
help me to celebrate their lives, to affirm them,
and help me to remember that they are Yours more than ours.

When I do not know where to turn,
may I turn to you, O God, in heartfelt prayer.

I believe, my God, that from the beginning you have been with me, and in times of pain and difficulty you have often carried me. And I trust that as it was in the beginning, so it is now and will be always. I offer this prayer in the name of Jesus. Amen.[4]

Prayer of a Single Parent

In this short prayer, express dependence upon God for strength, companionship, and guidance in the often difficult and solitary vocation of being a single parent. Pray with trust that your God is a God of compassion, and will not test you beyond your strength.

> My God, help me to be both Mother and Father to my children. Keep me healthy and strong on those days when I am weak. Remind me to love them in the same way that you have shown that special love for me. Amen.[5]

Blessing of a New Baby

African peoples believe in life as the greatest of all gifts. A new member of the family or clan increases its life force, brings a promise of prosperity, and guarantees its ultimate survival.

> May your face be radiant like the rising sun.
> May your smile brighten the cloudy sky.
> May your cries always find a gentle response.
>
> May your first steps fall on firm ground.
> May your first sounds speak peace like the morning dew.
> May your first teeth be as white as Kilimanjaro's peak.
> May your ears be open to the bidding of your mother and father.
> May your hands perform good works for your family and clan.
> May your head bow low in respect before your elders.
> Amen![6]

A Mother's Blessing

One of the dearest joys in a mother's life is the ability to give her children what is good. What a privilege for the woman of faith to pray that her child be filled with the choicest blessings of God!

The joy of God be in thy face,
Joy to all who see thee,
The circle of God around thy neck,
Angels of God shielding thee,
Angels of God shielding thee.
Joy of night and day be thine,
Joy of sun and moon be thine,
Joy of men and women be thine,
each land and sea thou goest,
each land and sea thou goest.
Be every season happy for thee,
Be every season bright for thee,
Be everyone glad for thee.
Thou beloved one of my breast.
Thou beloved one of my heart.[7]

Parents' Baptism Prayer

In the preparations for Baptism, perhaps you received material from your parish describing this unique moment in the life of your child. Read prayerfully the explanations and the prayers given. Who in your family and faith community will support you as you take up the privileged role of initiating your son or daughter into the faith?

Promise yourself that you will call on them when you need support and help. Give thanks for the gift of this extended family of faith. Pray for light and grace to live your calling with generosity and with joy.

Creator God, you love us with motherly and fatherly love.
With joy and grateful hearts,
we give thanks for this new life entrusted to us.
Shower abundant blessings on her/him
as we celebrate her/his baptism.
Daily, may she/he grow in the likeness
of your dear child Jesus
in communion with you and all that you love.
In Jesus' name we pray. Amen.

A Prayer to Grow in Love

To grow in love is to be open to the gift of God's love seeping into our way of seeing, our way of knowing, our way of caring and responding, our way of reverencing the other. As the love of God more and more finds a home in us, we become for others witnesses and reminders of God's love.

All holy One, your name is Love.
I pray for the greatest of your gifts,
the gift of a loving heart—
for my spouse and my children,
for my extended family,
for the worldwide family of men, women, and children
who share time and space on this planet Earth.
Shape my heart to be a vessel

for your unbounded love
that I may generously share that love
with the other.
In Jesus' name, I pray. Amen.

Prayer for the Gift of a Child

I have witnessed firsthand the angst of many a couple and in particular of women, faced with the prospect of childlessness, yet desiring to have children of their own. Their prayers and supplications are often expressed in images, symbols, and metaphors pregnant with meaning. They resemble the prayer of Hannah (1 Samuel 1:1–18).

God of life, deep source of all life,
Unlock the sacred grove of life within me.
Remove from me the humiliation of childlessness.
Do not give my enemies cause to rejoice over me.

God of life, deep source of all life,
Plant a seed of life in the fertile depth of my womb.
Make the egg of life grow unharmed in the moist bed of my womb.
Do not allow the fragile thread of life to break in my womb.

God of life, deep source of all life,
May the sweet cry of life echo from deep within my womb.
May I know the joyful pain of childbirth.
May my neighbors gather around me to sing a song of new life.

God of life, deep source of all life,
May my bosom be a restful place for the fruit of my womb.
May my breasts suckle the delicate fruit of my own labor.
May my back know the joy of carrying the gentle load of my womb.[8]

A Prayer to Become Pregnant

As you offer this prayer, ask God to quicken the life-giving Spirit within you. Pray for consolation and courage. Pray for the gift of hope. Let your heart speak.

Your wife will be like a fruitful vine within your
house;
your children will be like olive shoots around your
table. (Psalm 128:3)

Creator God,
I pray to you in the company of Mary, Mother of your Beloved Child, Jesus,
in the company of Sarah and of Elizabeth—who for long years knew the pain of childlessness,
in the company of all holy women who have brought new life into the world
and nurtured and cared for their children.
The deepest desire of my heart is that our love will be fruitful,
that you will give us children with whom to share our love.
Within my woman's body,

create new life, just as you knitted my own body
within my mother's womb.
Give joy to my husband and to me,
that the love we share may overflow into new life.
You, my God, are the Giver of all life.
I place all my trust in you. Amen.

Prayer to St. Gerard during Pregnancy

St. Gerard, holy intercessor for mothers and babies, please pray for us during this time of our pregnancy. I feel this blessed life growing within me, and I am filled with praise for our Wondrous Creator—a God who gives life, and then entrusts us to nurture and nourish it. I think about our Blessed Mother, bearer of the very Son of God, and of my own mother, who bore me in loving faithfulness. My prayer is that God protects this baby; that we have a safe and healthy pregnancy and delivery; and that this child and all our family grow in living faith until we find our place among God's Communion of Saints in everlasting life.[9]

Remembering the Saints in Our Lives

Take a few quiet moments to step away from the busyness of the day, from your worries and anxieties. Think about those who have gone before you on the journey of life. How did their faith touch you? Specifically, can you recall any concrete events, particularly times of suffering, when difficulty seemed to be overwhelming? How was the faith of your family or close friends expressed? In your own living, do you see any echoes of their faith in you? Give thanks, and invite one or more of these persons to pray with you a favorite prayer.

Companion God,
always with me, ever faithful.
In your loving providence,
you open your hand and give all that we need.
My life is blessed with so many
whose faith and trust support me
especially in times of darkness and struggle.
I give you thanks, my God,
for ______________________________
(Here you may name your "personal saints.")
They are messengers of your wisdom, your
compassion, your love.
My grateful heart sings your praise!

A Simple Litany of Saints

How often in my conversations do I refer to persons in my life, both living and deceased, who have influenced me, supported and challenged me, loved and cared for me. These are my personal saints; take time to recall their names, perhaps to speak with them, and give thanks.

For all the saints
who went before us
who have spoken to our hearts
and touched us with your fire,
we praise you, O God.

For all the saints
who live beside us
whose weaknesses and strengths
are woven in our own,
we praise you, O God.

For all the saints
who live beyond us
who challenge us
to change the world with them,
we praise you, O God.[10]

Prayer for Our Friends

Reflect on one of life's greatest gifts—the gift of friendship. Recall those who have been friends and companions over the years. What gifts and graces did they bring into your life? Recall those closest to you now. Give thanks for what they bring to this segment of your journey. Pray for their well-being, their happiness, and their peace. Pray that you may be a blessing to them.

Faithful friends are a sturdy shelter:
whoever finds one has found a treasure.
Faithful friends are beyond price;
no amount can balance their worth. (Sirach 6:14–15)

Jesus, companion and friend,
you shared your earthly life with so many.
Your touch brought healing;
your words spoke peace.
And as you witnessed to God's great love,
you sought friends to be at your side,
to walk with you on the journey.

I give you thanks today for the friends who walk with me—
(you may want to name some of them . . .)

those who deepen my joy and share my pain,
those who offer counsel and provide comfort,
those who stand with me in troubled times,
those who know me and love me,
oftentimes better than I know and love myself.
They show me your face.
Teach me to love unselfishly,
to give and not to count the cost,
to be a blessing to my friends,
as they are blessing to me.
As we walk life's roads with you,
may our hearts burn within us
that graced by your presence,
we may grow into that full stature
which you desire for all your beloved sisters and brothers.
In your name, Jesus, we pray. Amen.

Blessings

We are all familiar with blessings—prayers that ask God's favor upon another. In these three short blessings, two from scripture, the third from the Celtic tradition, I pray that God surround the other with good gifts—peace, kindness, grace.

Ancient Biblical Blessing

The Lord bless you and keep you;
The Lord make his face to shine upon you,
and be gracious to you;
The Lord lift up his countenance upon you,
and give you peace. (Numbers 6:24–26)

Early Christian Blessing

The peace of God,
which surpasses all understanding,
keep your hearts and minds in the knowledge and
love of God
and of God's son Jesus Christ our Lord;
and the blessing of God almighty,
the Father, the Son, and the Holy Spirit,
be among you and remain with you always.[11]

Irish Blessing

May the road rise to meet you.
May the wind be always at your back.
May the sun shine warm upon your face.
May the rains fall soft upon your fields.
Until we meet again
May God hold you in the hollow of his hand.

Words That Invite Reflection

When we look for a model of what it means to be human, or how we can be our best selves and give the best of who we are to the other in the gift of loving, we need look no further than Jesus, a man in love, the one who enfleshed the compassion of God.

Christ, a Man in Love

It was the *Word* that was made flesh. Not only did [Jesus] take our sorrows to himself, but he gave

the delight and the happiness that *he is,* to our humanness.
No man [sic] ever enjoyed life as much as he did. He gathered up the color, sound, touch, meaning, of everything about him and united it all to the most exquisite sensitiveness, the most pure capacity for delight.
Most people know the sheer wonder that goes with falling in love, how not only does everything in heaven and earth become new, but the lover becomes new as well. . . . The heart is enlarged; there is more sympathy, more warmth in it than ever before. . . . Christ on earth was a man in love. His love gave life to all loves. He was Love itself. He infused life with all the grace of its outward and inward joyfulness, with all its poetry and song, with all the gaiety and laughter and grace.[12]

The Really Real . . . Saving Love

What is the nature of the Really Real? Jesus' response is that the Really Real is generous, forgiving, saving love. How does a good man [sic] behave? The good man [sic] is a person who is captivated by the joy and wonder of God's promise. In the end, will life triumph over death or death over life? Jesus is perfectly confident: The kingdom of his Father cannot be vanquished, not even by death. [13]

And so Jesus is our true Mother in nature by our first creation, and he is our true Mother in grace by his taking our created nature. All the lovely works and all the sweet loving offices of beloved motherhood are appropriated to the second person . . .

. . . The Mother's service is nearest, readiest and surest: nearest because it is most natural, readiest because it is most loving, and surest because it is truest. No one ever might or could perform this office fully, except only him. [14]

Where there is no love, put love and you will find love.[15]

For the Wider Human Family

"The love of Christ urges us on . . ." wrote Paul in his Second Letter to the Corinthians (2 Corinthians 5:14). Faithful disciples of Jesus cannot stand on the sidelines as members of the human family are suffering, whether from poverty, war, prejudice, the fragmentation of society, or tensions within the Church. The prayers in this section stretch our hearts, as concerns for the human family claim our attention and call for response.

Aware of the overwhelming needs of the human family, I cry out for God's help to change the way I see, think, act. May God make me an instrument to heal the woundedness of our world, and to labor for peace and unity.

Prayer for the Unity of the Human Family

These simple words convey the fundamental message—one earth, one family. We pray for peace to work together and overcome whatever barriers divide us—economic, racial, cultural, religious, etc.

Almighty God, who are mother and father to us all,
Look upon your planet Earth divided:
Help us to know that we are all your children;
That all nations belong to one great family,
And all of our religions lead to you.
Multiply our prayers in every land
Until the whole Earth becomes your congregation,
United in your love.
Sustain our vision of a peaceful future
And give us strength to work unceasingly
To make that vision real. Amen.[16]

God's Vision

This prayer invites reflection on a world where suffering has been transformed by the loving response of those who share God's vision.

Give us, O God, a vision of your world as love would make it;
a world where the weak are protected and none go hungry;
a world where benefits are shared, so that everyone
can enjoy them;
a world whose different people and cultures live with tolerance
and mutual respect;
a world where peace is built with justice,
and justice is fired with love;

Lord Jesus Christ, give us the courage to build.
Amen.[17]

Prayer for a Compassionate Heart

This prayer calls us to awareness of the reality of suffering in the world and of the response of those who care and who want to make things different. A group like a social-responsibility committee may wish to use this prayer at the beginning or the end of its meeting.

Defender of Women and Children,
Out of pain and rejection
You molded Jesus' heart of compassion,
And caused Him to rise up
On behalf of outcasts and sinners.
Open our hearts to the despised
And rejected ones of the world,
That, surrounding them
With the intensity of your love,
We bring them into Your household
To be cherished by You forever;
Friend and Advocate of the lost,
Liberating One.
Amen.[18]

Prayer for an Inclusive Love

Who can know the mind of God? In a time when society is becoming more and more diverse, when the marvels of technology allow us to see and hear and even experience the diversity of cultures, civilizations, religions, I pray for an open mind, an expansive heart to reverence all that God's creative word calls into being.

Eternal God, whose image lies in the hearts of all
people,
We live among peoples whose ways are different from
ours,
Whose faiths are foreign to us,
Whose tongues are unintelligible to us.
Help us to remember that you love all people with
your great love,
That all religion is an attempt to respond to you,
That the yearnings of other hearts are much like
our own
and are known to you.
Help us to recognize you in the words of truth, the
things of beauty,
The actions of love about us.
We pray through Christ, who is a stranger to no one
land more than another,
And to every land no less than to another.[19]

God—Let Me Be Aware

Unless I see, unless I become aware, unless my consciousness of the other grows and deepens, I will not embrace fully Jesus' great command "to love as I have loved you." I pray to see as God sees.

Stab my soul fiercely with others' pain.
Let me walk seeing horror and stain.
Let my hands, groping, find other hands.
Give me the heart that divines, understands,
Give me the courage, wounded, to fight.
Flood me with knowledge,
Drench me in light.
Please—keep me eager just to do my share.
God—let me be aware![20]

Remembering Dorothy Day

Dorothy Day is one of the great American pioneers and prophets calling us to serve those who are poor, and to labor for peace and harmony in our world. Her life and work continue to speak today. I pray that I may grow in her spirit of compassion and generosity.

Friend and partner of the poor,
Guiding spirit for the Catholic Worker,
Home always open to the unwanted.
Early, often lonely, witness
in the cause of peace and conscience.
Eloquent pattern of gospel simplicity—
Dorothy Day, disciple of the Lord:
May we continue your gift of self to the needy
and your untiring work for peace![21]

God's Bounty, a Reminder

It is easy to pray in thanksgiving for God's bounty. In this prayer, I remember those who lack food, shelter, jobs, and those who suffer in any way. I pray to turn my gratitude to deeds of caring.

O God, when I have food, help me to remember the hungry;
When I have work, help me to remember the jobless;
When I have a home, help me to remember those who have no home at all;
When I am without pain, help me to remember those who suffer;
And remembering, help me to destroy my
complacency; bestir my compassion,
And be concerned enough to help, by word and deed,
those who cry out for what we take for granted.[22]

Prayers for Migrants and for Refugees

In the following two prayers, one for migrants and the other for refugees, I am reminded of the pilgrim Christ. I remember the first settlers in my own country, my ancestors. I pray for a welcoming heart and for light that as a nation greatly blessed, we may wisely and compassionately address the challenges of migration in our own times.

FOR MIGRANTS

O Christ, pilgrim before birth,
you made your life a march of meetings with others.

Not knowing where to rest your head,
you wanted every person, all of us pilgrims,
to have hope.

We bring to you the needs of all migrants:
Give them a place that will nourish them
and will make them strong of heart, firm in their
identity.
Help them to live in justice,
in solidarity, and in peace.
In your love see that they are welcomed.
All are made in your image,
all are bound toward community
with sisters and brothers in the faith.

May they not walk more than necessary,
and when they halt
may their walking not be in vain.
May we migrants all be blessed as the world is
blessed.
Amen.[23]

FOR REFUGEES

O Jesus, I pray for those who wander far from their
homeland
and live the lives of migrants.
They are our brothers and sisters,
refugees who flee from violence,
families on the road because of poverty.
None of them know where to arrive.

All of them need your help!
You know them
for you yourself experienced the hard days of exile
together with Mary and Joseph.

Our migrant sisters and brothers need your light
to uncover the empty promises that frequently attract them.
They need your church to remind them of their obligations,
often forgotten in their daily sufferings.
They need your help
to ennoble and to confirm them as Christians in their work.

Heart of Jesus, bless the migrants,
and fill their lives with the love of God
from whom all good things come.

Defend them from danger.
Make strong their faith
to seek happiness not only in this world, but also for eternal life.
As pilgrims, as the church itself,
May they reach the heavenly city and be with you forever.
Amen.[24]

For Life

Prayer for Reverence of Life

Life in its fullness is what God desires. Within the human family, life issues assume enormous significance. We pray that all life be respected and reverenced. Life issues are a seamless garment.

Almighty God, giver of all that is good,
We thank you for the precious gift of human life.

For life in the womb, coming from your creative power.
For the life of children, making us glad with their
freshness and promise.
For the life of young people, hoping for a better world.
For the life of the handicapped and disabled, teaching us humility.
For the life of the elderly, witnessing the ageless
values of patience and wisdom.
Like Blessed Mary, may we always say "yes" to your gift.
May we defend it and promote it from conception to its natural end
and bring us at last, O Father, to eternal life
in Jesus Christ our Lord. Amen.[25]

A Prayer to Abolish the Death Penalty

I pray for a forgiving heart, for the grace to be like Christ who prayed for his executioners and for those crucified with him. And I pray for our country—that as a society, we may turn from the path of violence and vengeance—and work for the renewal and rehabilitation of all persons.

God of compassion,
You let your rain fall on the just and the unjust.
Expand and deepen our hearts
so that we may love as you love,
even those among us who have caused the greatest pain
by taking life.
For there is in our land a great cry for vengeance
as we fill up death row and kill the killers
in the name of justice, in the name of peace.

Jesus, our brother,
You suffered execution at the hands of the state
but you did not let hatred overcome you.
Help us to reach out to victims of violence
so that our enduring love may help them heal.
Holy Spirit of God,
You strengthen us in the struggle for justice.
Help us to work tirelessly
for the abolition of state-sanctioned death
and to renew our society in its very heart
so that violence will be no more.
Amen.[26]

For Peace

Bearing Witness to Peace

I know that peace must first dwell within each human heart, and that true peace within the family of nations will come when peace grows in individual human hearts. I pray to be an instrument of that peace. This prayer reflects the spirit of St. Francis of Assisi's prayer, "Lord, make me an instrument of your peace."

Lord God, we come to you in our need.
Create in us an awareness of the massive forces
that threaten our world today.
Give us a sense of urgency
to activate the forces of goodness, of justice, of love,
and of peace.

Where there is armed conflict,
let us stretch our arms to our brothers and sisters.
Where there is abundance,
let there be simple lifestyle and sharing.

Where there is poverty,
let there be dignified living and constant striving for
just structures.
Where there are wounds of division,
let there be unity and wholeness.
Help us to be committed to the building of your
kingdom.

Not seeking to be cared for,
but to care.
Not expecting to be served,
but to place ourselves in the service of others.
Not aspiring to be materially secure,
but to place our security in your love.

Teach us your spirit.
Only in loving imitation of you
can we discover the healing springs of life
that will bring new birth to our world.[27]

Prayer for the Decade of Nonviolence

The General Assembly of the United Nations declared the years 2001–2010 to be the International Decade for a Culture of Peace and Non-violence for the Children of the World. Twenty Nobel Peace Prize laureates originated this idea. In this prayer, I pledge to give myself to this work, in every area of my life.

I bow to the sacred in all creation.
May my spirit fill the world with beauty and wonder.
May my mind seek truth with humility and openness.
May my heart forgive without limit.
May my love for friend, enemy and outcast be without measure.
May my needs be few and my living simple.
May my actions bear witness to the suffering of others.
May my hands never harm a living being.
May my steps stay on the journey of justice.

May my tongue speak for those who are poor without
fear of the powerful.
May my prayers rise with patient discontent until no
child is hungry.
May my life's work be a passion for peace and
nonviolence.
May my soul rejoice in the present moment
May my imagination overcome death and despair
with new possibility.
And may I risk reputation, comfort and security to
bring this hope to the children.[28]

Prayer for Peace and Justice

This prayer to the Holy Spirit begs for the needs of our world—for justice and for peace—using familiar and vivid images from the scriptures. The classic images are relevant today.

Holy Spirit, it is time.
The children are hungry,
and the poor can no longer plant hope.

Your promise
to fill the poor with good things
and the rich sent empty away
goes unfulfilled.
It is an embarrassment,
a laughingstock,
a mockery of sacred promise.
Now overtake our hearts with your fire.

On earth let the flame of justice
leap wildly.
Release in us
a brilliant blaze of compassion.
Let the fires burn away
all pettiness, greed, selfishness,
and lust for security.
Let embers of kindness fill the land.

Whoever holds a debt, it will be forgiven.
Whoever is rich will give half away:
land returned to the peasant,
prison doors thrown open,
military budgets dissolved,
a cup of water given in Jesus' name.
Again. Again. And yet again.
Amen.[29]

For the Church

Twenty-first-century citizens live in a highly active media environment. Even the Church becomes a daily subject for reporting—its life and legacy, its controversies and challenges, its weaknesses and its strengths. We implore God's providential care for the Church, that the living Body of Christ become all that it is called to be.

Prayer for the Church

Concern for the life and vitality of the Church remains a constant through all of history. Believers seek God's help, relying on the Spirit of God, the very soul of the Church, dwelling deep within.

Gracious Father,
we pray to you for your holy Catholic Church.
Fill it with your truth.
Keep it in your peace.
Where it is corrupt, reform it.
Where it is in error, correct it.
Where it is right, defend it.
Where it is in want, provide for it.
Where it is divided, reunite it;
for the sake of your Son, our Savior Jesus Christ.[30]

For the Unity of the Church

In this prayer from ages past, we recognize the same issues that challenge the Church today. We pray Jesus' prayer, "that all may be one."

O God, source of perfect unity, pour out your grace upon your Church at prayer. Heal the divisions and mistrust that past years have wrought among your children. We pray without ceasing for conversion of heart and a deeper faithfulness to the gospel. We pray for a closer relationship with Christ Jesus who prayed, "that all may be one." Fill us with a desire to unite ourselves to his prayer of unity. May we live as one, as you are one, Father, Son and Holy Spirit, now and forever. Amen.[31]

Prayer Remembering Blessed Pope John XXIII

For the renewal of the Church.

In the life and example of "Good Pope John," we recognize a faithful and humble witness, a true shepherd and pastor concerned for the life and growth of the Church of Jesus Christ. We pray to share in his spirit, as we face the new and often unexpected challenges of our twenty-first-century Church.

We give you thanks and praise, dear God,
For blessing us with blessed John,
Peasant by birth and by choice,
Servant of your servants,
Worker for peace on earth,
Brother to all people of good will.
In baptism, he put on Christ:
To love the world, to be of good cheer,
To undo the arrogant and lift up the helpless,
To speak new words to the weary.

How he lived that gospel word—
"Be cunning as serpents,
Simple as doves."
How he preached that Gospel word—
Not announcing doom
But in love rushing to the world's side.
Raise up in us, your church,
The spirit that filled blessed John:
Modest for ourselves but bold for you,

Setting off unafraid for places we have not gone before,
And ever seeking our peace in your will.

This we ask in Jesus' name,
Our good shepherd who is Lord
For ever and ever. Amen.
Good Pope John, pray for us![32]

Words That Invite Reflection

As I continue growing toward fuller life, toward a deeper awareness of the oneness of the human family, my heart expands. I am touched by the needs of the larger human family. Concerns for those who are poor, those deprived of human rights, those thrust into the nightmare of war, those driven from their homeland—these and so many other tragedies cry out for redress. They touch my heart and challenge me to respond.

The Call to Serve

Jesus has no body on earth but yours.
Yours are the eyes through which his compassion looks out on the world.
Yours are the feet with which he is to go about doing good.
And yours are the hands with which he is to bless us now.[33]

The Gift of Our Lives

We will need courage
We will need energy
We will need vision
We will need to be at ease
with ourselves and our decisions.

Above all, like the psalmist
We will need to keep "our eyes fixed on the Lord, our God."

Until God lets us rest and then we will know
As we have always known
That the effort was worth
The gift of our lives,
The best of our years,
The length of our days.[34]

Our Time Is Now

Thank God our time is now when wrong
Comes up to meet us everywhere,
Never to leave us till we take
The longest stride of soul folks ever took.
Affairs are now soul size. . . .
The enterprise
Is exploration into God.
Where are you making for?
It takes
So many thousand years to wake,
But will you wake for pity's sake . . .[35]

Charity Begins Today . . .

Charity begins today. Today somebody is suffering, today somebody is in the street, today somebody is hungry. Our work is for today, yesterday has gone, tomorrow has not yet come—today, we have only today to make Jesus known, loved, served, fed, clothed, sheltered, etc. Today—do not wait for tomorrow. Tomorrow might not come. Tomorrow we will not have them if we do not feed them today. [36]

Christ in the Stranger's Guise

I saw a stranger today.
I put food for him in the eating-place,
And drink in the drinking-place,
And music in the listening-place.
In the Holy Name of the Trinity
He blessed myself and my house,
My goods and my family.
And the lark said in her warble,
Often, often, often
Goes Christ in the stranger's guise
O, oft and oft and oft,
Goes Christ in the stranger's guise. [37]

Peace Pledge

Just for today . . .
I will live in peace with God, my neighbor and myself.
I will believe that world peace is possible.

I will not be a party to pessimism or join the ranks of the indifferent.
I will love my enemies. I will pray for them;
I will try to see our differences from their point of view.
I will disarm myself of rage by extending my hand in help and forgiveness.
I will know that peace is the child of justice—that
peace is more than the absence of war.
I will plant the seed of justice in this global village, in my city,
in my neighborhood, in my family and in my heart.
I will test my love of peace by doing one act for peace.
I will stand with Christ the Peacemaker, who lives and
reigns forever and ever.
Amen.[38]

There are people in the world so hungry, that God cannot appear to them except in the form of bread.[39]

Into each of our lives Jesus comes as the bread of life—to be eaten, to be consumed by us. Then he comes as the hungry one, the other, hoping to be fed with the bread of our life, our hearts lovingly, and our hands serving.[40]

Never doubt that a small group of thoughtful, committed citizens can change the world. Indeed, it is the only thing that ever has.[41]

CHAPTER FOUR

Praying My Sufferings and Struggles

The Dark Times

No one of us journeys through life without encountering dark days and hard times, struggles and stress. Serious illness, financial crisis, loss of employment, broken relationships, betrayal—when situations like these crash into our lives, we feel alarm, fear, anxiety, perhaps depression. What is your response? Do you turn to God and cry out for relief? Do you blame God for "causing" this suffering? Do you consider suffering a punishment from God? Be in touch with your feelings so that you may turn to God with honesty and truth. The prayers in this section give voice to a variety of human experiences.

Psalm 61:1–5, 8

Quiet your spirit, attending to the Holy One dwelling deep within you. Let the tenderness of God enfold you. Let the strength of God bear you up. Rest in the embrace of love, the love that never abandons, but remains with you. Know the comforting presence of God.

Hear my cry, O God;
listen to my prayer.
From the end of the earth I call to you,
when my heart is faint.

Lead me to the rock
that is higher than I;
for you are my refuge,
a strong tower against the enemy.

Let me abide in your tent forever,
find refuge under the shelter of your wings.
For you, O God, have heard my vows;
you have given me the heritage
of those who fear your name.

So I will always sing praises to your name,
as I pay my vows day after day.

"Freed"—A Prayer to Christ

When I experience difficult times, I turn to Christ Jesus who walked before me through the darkness. Jesus, companion, walks with me, upholding me in the dark times.

O Christ,
you take upon yourself all our burdens
so that,
freed of all that weighs us down,
we can constantly begin anew to walk,
with lightened step,
from worry towards trusting,
from the shadows towards the clear flowing waters,
from our own will
towards the vision of the coming kingdom.
And then we know,
though we hardly dared hope so,
that you offer to make every human being
a reflection of your face.[1]

Father, Forgive

The following words are inscribed on the prayer panels at the site of the ruins of the cathedral in Coventry, England. The cathedral was destroyed in a 1940 bombing raid on the city. The new cathedral, St. Michael's, was built adjacent to the ruins. The people of the city preserved the ruins as an ever-present reminder of the horror of war and the daily challenge to labor for peace and reconciliation. This continues to be our challenge, too. We pray for forgiveness in our own times, for the failures of society as well as of individuals.

The HATRED which divides nation from nation, race from race, class from class,
Father, forgive
The COVETOUS desires of men and nations to possess what is not their own,
Father, forgive
The GREED which exploits the labors of men and lays waste the earth,
Father, forgive
Our ENVY of the welfare and happiness of others
Father, forgive
Our INDIFFERENCE to the plight of the homeless and the refugee,
Father, forgive
The LUST which uses for ignoble ends the bodies of men and women,
Father, forgive.
The PRIDE which leads us to trust in ourselves and not in God,
Father, forgive.

Be kind to one another, tenderhearted, forgiving one another, as God in Christ forgave you.[2]

For Reconciliation

All around me, I see signs of brokenness, alienation, hostility—between persons, within families, within and among nations. Jesus came as healer, as reconciler, as unifier. Where is the brokenness in my life? In my relationships? Ask Jesus for the grace of a forgiving heart.

> Lord God,
> out of your great love for the world,
> you reconciled earth to heaven
> through your only-begotten Son our Savior.
> In the darkness of our sins
> we fail to love one another as we should;
> please pour your light into our souls
> and fill us with your tenderness
> that we may embrace our friends in you
> and our enemies for your sake,
> in a bond of mutual affection.
> We make our prayer through the same Christ our Lord.[3]

A Prayer at the End of a Hard Day: Isaiah 54:10–11

Take a few moments to name the frustrations, the struggles, and the feelings you are aware of deep in your soul. Ask God to be with you and to help you trust in this difficult situation. Ask the Holy One to enfold you, to uphold you, and to bring light into your darkness, to give you the strength you need and desire.

For the mountains may depart and the hills be
removed,
but my steadfast love shall not depart from you,
and my covenant of peace shall not be removed,
says the Lord, who has compassion on you.

O afflicted one, storm-tossed, and not comforted,
I am about to set your stones in antimony,
and lay your foundations with sapphires.

Out of the Depths I Cry . . .

At times, the burdens of life overwhelm us: death of a loved one, critical illness, severe financial crises, other suffering so difficult to bear. Though we may be tempted to turn away from God, life's tragedies are always an invitation to find God in the midst of the suffering. This scripture text and subsequent reflection from the great medieval mystic Julian of Norwich remind us of God's presence even in the darkest hour.

> I have said these things to you while I am still with you. But the Advocate, the Holy Spirit, whom the Father will send in my name, will teach you everything, and remind you of all that I have said to you. Peace I leave with you; my peace I give to you. I do not give to you as the world gives. Do not let your hearts be troubled, and do not let them be afraid. (John 14:25–27)

> And so our good Lord answered to all the questions and doubts which I could raise, saying most comfortingly in this fashion: I will make all things well, I shall make all things well, I may make all things well, and I will make all things well and I can make all things well; and you will see that yourself, that all things will be well.[4]

Prayer from the Darkness

There are times when I am weighed down by what seem to be enormous difficulties—serious sickness, a financial crisis, fraying or broken relationships. The darkness overwhelms me. Place your heart in the compassionate heart of your God and ask for healing.

My God, I have no words to name the pain within me.
A deep darkness drenches my soul.
No light. No hope. No out.
From my mother's womb, O God, you know me.
Be with me; mend, make whole again my torn and
  broken spirit.
Lift me up, that this cross of suffering
may become for me the tree of life,
that sacred Tree whose outstretched arms embrace me
and draw me to your heart.
Even in this pain, may I find your blessing. Amen.

Prayer after a Miscarriage or Stillbirth

Suffering the loss of a child is a pain so difficult to understand, to bear. Hand over your pain to the One who is author of life. Cry out your suffering, perhaps even feelings of alienation and anger. God, who knows your heart, weeps with you. Pray to trust God's love even in this unspeakable sadness.

My God, Creator God, why have you forsaken me?
Compassionate One,
I come to you with a heart of unspeakable sadness.
You called back to yourself the child of my womb.
The miracle of new life is not to be for us at this time.
I beg you, heal the deep wound we feel;
touch our hearts with the balm of your loving
  kindness.
Help us, day by day, to take another step in hope
and to find in this pain and loss,
some sign of your blessing.
In faith, we know that you now embrace (him/her)
  with profound love.
He/she lives an even fuller life with you.
In faith, we believe; yet our hearts so deeply grieve
  this loss.
Be with us, holy God, that through this mystery of
  life-and-death
we may come to accept whatever gifts you send
and even in the suffering, draw closer to you,
who love us more than we can ever imagine.

If it be your will, in your chosen time,
we pray that you will make us fruitful again with new life,
new life that you trust us to nurture and care for.

In the name of Jesus, your own Beloved Child, we pray. Amen.

Prayer for Healing

In times of illness, especially unexpected serious illness, people of faith turn to their God, to those who can intercede with God. This prayer for healing begs the intercession of Dorothy Stang, S.N.D. de N., a contemporary servant and martyr. She was murdered in Brazil in 2005 for her active ministry on behalf of peasant farmers and the preservation of the rain forests.

Blessed are You, Holy Creator,
Source of all that is good,
beautiful and whole.
Where wholeness is
splintered or shattered,
goodness damaged or marred,
and beauty bruised or broken,
we ask for healing and deep peace.
Be healing balm for this world:
for all people, creatures,
places, events, and for
the environment.

We welcome the touch of
your Healing love
and Gentle Presence.
Inspired by Dorothy Stang,
your servant and martyr,
we pray in communion
with all the saints in glory,
through Christ our Lord. Amen.[5]

A Prayer to Accept My Diminishment

Contemporary culture glorifies the culture of youth. The wisdom of years, however, speaks a different word: the goodness of the total life cycle, from birth to diminishment, death, and new life. I pray to embrace my own life cycle and the particular stage where I find myself in the journey. I recall the words of Francis of Assisi: "Praised be my Lord for our sister, the death of the body, from which no one escapes."

Jesus, who never grew old, it is not easy for any of us to face old age.
It is fine to be young, attractive, strong.
Old age reminds us of weakness and dependence on others.
But to be your disciple means accepting weakness and interdependence.
Because of you we can rejoice in weakness in ourselves,
and be tender to it in others.[6]

Words That Invite Reflection

When the days are dark, we seek consolation and strength; we look to the wisdom of the scriptures, of those who have gone before us. Our faith is the firm ground on which we stand. The gospels show us Jesus, a man of compassion, feeling human pain. We remember that Jesus wept and lamented in face of suffering.

A Reflection on Divine Sorrow

In scripture we find a God who identifies with the pain and suffering of the human family and of individual persons. The images of Jesus in the gospels show him to be a man of deep feeling—compassion for the widow of Nain at the loss of her son, his tears at the tomb of his friend Lazarus, Jesus' weeping over the city of Jerusalem. Such images from scripture can be a comfort to us. Jesus reveals to us his own heart; Jesus reveals to us the heart of his Abba. The texts which follow put us in touch with the compassion of God for all, for me.

> But Zion said, "The Lord has forsaken me,
> My Lord has forgotten me."
> Can a woman forget her nursing child,
> or show no compassion for the child of her womb?
> Even these may forget,
> yet I will not forget you.
> See, I have inscribed you on the palms of my hands;
> your walls are continually before me.
> (Isaiah 49:14–16)

For a brief moment I abandoned you,
but with great compassion I will gather you.
In overflowing wrath for a moment I
hid my face from you,
but with everlasting love I will have compassion on
you,
says the Lord, your Redeemer. (Isaiah 54:7–8)

When Mary came where Jesus was and saw him, she knelt at his feet and said to him, "Lord, if you had been here, my brother would not have died." When Jesus saw her weeping, and the Jews who came with her also weeping, he was greatly disturbed in spirit and deeply moved. He said, "Where have you laid him?" They said to him, "Lord, come and see." Jesus began to weep. So the Jews said, "See how he loved him!" (John 11:32–36)

St. Teresa's Bookmark

Let nothing disturb you, nothing affright you;
all things are passing, God never changes.
Patience attains all that it strives for;
one who possesses God finds nothing lacking:
God alone suffices.[7]

From moment to moment, one can bear much.[8]

I beg our Lord to help you find the rich treasure which His goodness has hidden at the very core of the pain that comes to you from His hand.[9]

> It is only the women whose eyes have been washed clear with tears who get the broad vision that makes them little sisters to all the world.[10]

Facing the Unknown: Decision Making

It is not smart to travel without a road map to an unknown destination. Nor is it easy for us to take the right steps, make the "right" decisions when we don't see clearly where we are headed. Such experiences are not uncommon and perhaps are more common in certain stages of life. In prayer, we place our confusion, our muddled state of mind before the God who is all truth and light, and who desires that each person find fulfillment in life.

God of Inner Knowing

There are times in my life journey when I feel lost—I'm at an unfamiliar place without a road map or compass to set a clear direction. Pray that experience; let God hear your questions; ask for light to know the way.

God of Inner Knowing,
Within my heart I have many questions
about who I am, who you are
and how we blend into being.
My world is so full of distractions
that sometimes it's difficult
to distinguish my voice from yours;
my will from your will.
You once asked Joseph

to take Jesus and Mary to a foreign land,
to await your word.
I feel that you are now asking the same of me
and I pray for the same obedient faith of Joseph,
for it is only in risking the journey
that one discovers the wisdom
of inner knowing.[11]

The Faithfulness of God

My faith tells me that God is like a rock, a sturdy foundation on which I can always securely and confidently stand. The image is a way of describing the faithfulness of God. This prayer recognizes and trusts God's faithfulness.

May you be blessed forever, Lord, for not abandoning me
when I abandoned you.
May you be blessed forever, Lord, for offering your hand of love
in my darkest, most lonely moment.

May you be blessed forever, Lord, for putting up with such
a stubborn soul as mine.

May you be blessed forever, Lord, for loving me
more than I love myself.
May you be blessed forever, Lord, for continuing to pour out your blessings upon me,
even though I respond so poorly.

May you be blessed forever, Lord, for drawing out the
goodness in people,
including me.
May you be blessed forever, Lord,
for repaying our sins with your love.
May you be blessed forever, Lord, for being constant
and unchanging,
amidst all the changes in the world.
May you be blessed forever, Lord, for your countless
blessings on me
and on every creature in the world.[12]

Light

In this prayer, I turn to God who is light. I pray that I may trust God to bring light to my darkness; I pray also that I may be light for others who walk in darkness.

Shining God,
even the darkness is not dark to you.
Shine in our darkness, light of our lives.
When we walk in the gray gloom of confusion,
when pain drains all the color out of life,
when we are paralyzed by the darkness of fear,
shine in our darkness.

When we know that others are walking in the
darkness,
give us courage to be light for them.[13]

God's Call into the Future

I pray to trust God who calls me into the future, a future that I do not know. I pray for openness to what is new, believing that God will never test me beyond my strength.

God of our lives
you are always calling us
to follow you into the future,
inviting us to new ventures, new challenges,
new ways to care,
new ways to touch the hearts of all.
When we are fearful of the unknown, give us courage.
When we worry that we are not up to the task,
remind us that you would not call us
if you did not believe in us.

When we get tired
or feel disappointed with the way things are going,
remind us that you can bring change and hope
out of the most difficult situations.[14]

A Prayer of Self-Abandonment

The following is another prayer from the modern missionary-martyr Sister Dorothy Stang, who spent her life in service to the poor farmers of Brazil and as an advocate for the care of the earth, especially the Amazon rainforests. She adapted the words of Charles de Foucauld in this prayer of self-offering and made them her own, drawing up the concrete gift of her own life.

Father, Mother,
I abandon myself into your hands;
do with me what you will.
Whatever you may do,
I thank you.
I am ready for all, I accept all
that only your will be done in me
and in all your creatures.
I wish no more than this, O Lord.
Into your hands I commend my soul.
I offer it to you with
all the love of my heart
for I love you, Lord,
and so need to give myself
to surrender into your hands
without reserve
and with boundless confidence.
For you are my Father Mother.[15]

Bless Our Transitions

I ask God's blessing on all the transitions in my life, on all that is new. I pray that God will "go with us as we go."

Bless to us, O God,
the doors we open,
the thresholds we cross,
the roads that lie before us.
Go with us as we go
and welcome us home.[16]

Praying Our Worries

So often my worries are about the basic necessities of life—food, health, work, enough money, etc. I pray to trust God who loves me without measure, to trust, even when I am most anxious.

> Dear God, it is so hard for us not to be anxious.
> We worry about work and money,
> about food and health,
> about weather and crops,
> about war and politics,
> about loving and being loved.
> Show us how perfect love casts out fear.[17]

Words That Invite Reflection

These texts offer perspective on how we face uncertainties. Others have lived through similar experiences. I trust that I, too, will have strength to walk through this difficult time.

Trust in the Hard Times

> He (Jesus) did not say, "You shall not be tempest-tossed, you shall not be work-weary, you shall not be discomforted." But he said, "You shall not be overcome." God wants us to heed these words so that we shall always be strong in trust, both in sorrow and in joy.[18]

Live the Questions

Be patient toward all that is unsolved in your heart and try to love the questions. Do not seek the answers, which cannot be given. You would not be able to live them. Live everything. Live the questions now. Perhaps you will then gradually, without noticing it, live along some distant day into the answer.[19]

God Said, "I Thank You"

I saw God in an instant of time,
in my understanding,
and by this vision
I saw that God is present in all things . . .
And God said to me:
I thank you
for your service and your labor,
and especially in your youth.[20]

Encouragement in Prayer

For many times our trust is not complete; we are not sure whether God hears us, or so it seems, owing to our unworthiness, and we feel quite empty. How often are we barren and dry at prayer, sometimes seeming even more so when they are done. Yet this is only in our feelings and caused by our own folly, coming from weakness; I have felt as much myself . . . Our Lord is full of gladness and delight at our prayers;

he looks out for them, for he wants them longingly. For by means of his grace they make us grow like himself in condition as we are in kind; this is his blessed will. . . .[21]

Our Lives, a Wreath

So many things happen
in a day, in a year, in a life.
How are we to receive them
allow them
make them all fit?
One way perhaps is
to see of our lives a wreath

Finding the circle within
that has no beginning and no end

On which to arrange all things:
the separate, the opposite
even the unwanted

And make of them
a wholeness
a peace
and in due time
a true joy.[22]

"And remember, I am with you always, to the end of the age." (Matthew 20:28)

The feeling remains that God is on the journey, too.[23]

Vocation. It comes from the Latin *vocare,* to call, and means the work a person is called to by God. The place God calls you to is the place where your deep gladness and the world's deep hunger meet.[24]

People are like stained glass windows. They sparkle and shine when the sun is out, but when the darkness sets in their true beauty is revealed only if there is light within.[25]

Facing Death

Even in the face of death, the woman of faith clings to God's promise—"I am with you always." Death is the ultimate surrender; it is the doorway that opens into the fullness of life. The prayers and reflections that follow give voice to the faith and trust that live within us—even if at times, this faith and trust seem dormant.

Prayer about Diminishment

The words of this prayer become a meditation on the profound acceptance of our own diminishment—a journey into the heart of God.

When the signs of age begin to mark my body
(and still more when they touch my mind);
　　when the ill that is to diminish me or carry me off
　　strikes from without or is born within me;

when the painful moment comes
in which I suddenly awaken to the fact
that I am ill or growing old;
    And above all in that last moment
    when I feel I am losing hold of myself
    and am absolutely passive within the hands
    of the great, unknown forces that have formed
    me;
in all those dark moments, O God,
grant that I may understand that it is You
    (provided only my faith is strong enough)
who are painfully parting the fibers of my being
in order to penetrate to the very marrow of my
substance
and bear me away within Your substance.[26]

A Call to the Lord Jesus: Come!

These two brief prayers—one contemporary, the other from the sixteenth century—express the soul's longing for the face of God. The words recall the psalmist's cry: "As a deer longs for flowing streams, so my soul longs for you, O God" (Psalm 42:1).

Come, My Lord

Come, my Lord! Our darkness end!
Break the bonds of time and space.
All the power of evil rend
By the radiance of your face.

The laughing stars with joy attend:
Come, Lord Jesus! Be my end![27]

Welcome, My Beloved
Bridegroom and Lord, the longed-for hour has come!
It is time for us to see one another, my Beloved, my Master.
It is time for me to set out. Let us go.[28]

A Closer Walk with Thee

This familiar spiritual employs the simple image of walking with the Lord, walking ever closer with the Lord. Faithful believers know that life's daily journey rehearses them for that ultimate final journey crossing over "to thy kingdom shore."

I am weak but thou art strong;
Jesus, keep me from all wrong;
I'll be satisfied as long
As I walk, let me walk close to thee.
Through this world of toil and snares,
If I falter, Lord, who cares?
Who with me my burden shares?
None but thee, dear Lord, none but thee.

When my feeble life is o'er,
Time for me will be no more;
Guide me gently safely o'er
To thy kingdom shore, to thy shore.
Just a closer walk with thee,

Grant it, Jesus, is my plea,
Daily walking close to thee,
Let it be, dear Lord, let it be.[29]

A Reflection on the Approach of Death

In this spiritual, the recurring refrain declares that life on earth is not forever: "I ain't got long to stay here." Hear the comforting note sounded in the refrain: "steal away, steal away to Jesus . . . steal away home."

Steal away, steal away,
Steal away to Jesus!
Steal away, steal away home,
I ain't got long to stay here.

My Lord, he calls me,
He calls me by the thunder;
the trumpet sounds within my soul;
I ain't got long to stay here.

Green trees are bending,
poor sinners stand a trembling;
The trumpet sounds within my soul;
I ain't got long to stay here.

My Lord, he calls me,
he calls me by the lightning;
The trumpet sounds within my soul;
I ain't got long to stay here.[30]

Homecoming

The two following prayers express deep and profound faith. Let that faith strengthen and deepen your own faith. Pray the prayer slowly, reflectively. Ask the Spirit of God to pray within you; open your heart to receive the Spirit's gifts.

I believe there is Someone waiting for me, Waiting to say:
"Welcome Home!" Someone I have never seen, but
whom I will recognize in the depths of my heart
because He has lived there since the beginning of time.
Someone who has never doubted my return,
never failed to still my doubts about my return.
I believe there is Someone who knows me so intimately,
loves me so totally, that joy will spark spontaneously
when we reunite in the land of immortal Birth.
Tears will be wiped away;
Sadness and fear will disappear as mist when it meets the morning sun.
This is whom I seek, seeks me.
He has never left me alone.
For He is Self of my self,
Soul of my soul,
Life of my very life.[31]

Love Awaits Me

What will happen on the other side,
when all of me will have stumbled into eternity—
I don't know.
I only believe that LOVE awaits me.
I know that then,
all that remains of me must become poor and
weightless . . .

But don't think I'll despair. No, I believe.
I believe so much that a LOVE awaits me.

Don't speak to me of the glory and praise of the
Blessed Ones,
And don't speak to me of Angels, either!
All I can do is believe—believe stubbornly that a
LOVE awaits me.
Now that my hour is so near, what is there to say?
I can only smile.
What I have believed, I will believe even more as
death approaches.
As I take my leave, I walk toward LOVE, and into
LOVE I shall slowly fall.

If I die, don't weep for me. It's LOVE that has taken
me.
If I'm afraid—and why not?—simply remind me
that a Love—LOVE ITSELF—awaits me.
LOVE will completely open me to its joy, its light.

Yes, Abba! I am coming to You.

The wind, of which we know neither whence it comes
nor where it goes—
brings me toward YOUR LOVE.
It is YOUR LOVE that awaits me.[32]

Prayer to St. Joseph, for Those Who Watch

Our faith tradition honors Joseph as patron of a happy death. For those who keep vigil during the final journey of a loved one, Joseph is a faithful companion and strong support.

Good St. Joseph,
loving father of the child Jesus,
beloved spouse of Mary, his mother,
generations of believers turn to you as a faithful
provider.
We call upon you now for the grace of a happy death.
Accompany our loved one in this final journey;
Bring (him/her) the blessings of peace and joy.
Spare (him/her) any fear
that (s/he) may walk with eager step
into the arms of the One who welcomed (her/him) as
Beloved
in the waters of Baptism.
May we who watch
bring into this circle of care
the blessings of a faithful and loving presence,
ever mindful that the bonds which unite us are
stronger than death.

Be our advocate, holy Joseph,
in this and in all our needs. Amen.

Words That Invite Reflection

In life, there are many threshold moments, events by which we cross over to a "new place." While the event of death is the ultimate crossing over, each one of us crosses over many times in our life journey—we cross over from childhood to adolescence and then adulthood; we cross over from our family of origin to begin a new family or new way of life; we move from one neighborhood or city to another; from a full time job to retirement, and so on. In each instance, there is a "little death" of one way of life as we move into another. In the texts that follow, we find hope in the wisdom of fellow travelers.

For Those Who Grieve, Hope

"It is the will of him who sent me that I should lose nothing of what he has given me: rather, that I should raise it up on the last day" (John 6:39). That is our faith conviction about life in Christ. But we need to know what we do. *We counter the mystery of death with a greater mystery still, the mystery of risen life.* In the meantime there is grief, and nothing in Christian faith asks us to deny grief. We have known, all of us, someone who made an immense difference. We thank God for just that much. And we ask God for just enough strength to handle our grief.[33]

What It Means to "Stay Here and Watch"

> Unfortunately, in our society we keep death hidden. Few people have or seek the opportunity to witness the death of others. They would feel out of place as idle spectators. But this is perhaps because we do not have a Christian understanding of death in which the spectator is not idle at all but represents the active support and encouragement of the community.
> To witness death, however, places the same sort of demands on a person as the receiving of a confession of sin. It demands that one have come to terms rather radically with one's own approaching death as a dimension of life in the present.[34]

> And remember, I am with you always, to the end of the age. (Matthew 28:20)

> Listen! I am standing at the door, knocking; if you hear my voice and open the door, I will come in to you and eat with you, and you with me. (Revelation 3:20)

> I am now rejoicing in my sufferings for your sake, and in my flesh I am completing what is lacking in Christ's afflictions for the sake of his body, that is, the church. (Colossians 1:24)

PART TWO

An Invitation To Pray the Tradition

CHAPTER FIVE

The Scriptures

For Christians, sacred scripture, the Bible, is the sacred book. Christians refer to it as the "Word of God," and believe that this life-giving Word speaks to hearts and addresses lives. Revered by believers for thousands of years, the Word stands as a living Word; it remains ever ancient, ever new.

This library of sacred writings tells the story of generations of women and men who sought to understand the awesome—sometimes fearsome—mystery in their lives. Historical and cultural factors influenced the way our ancestors in the faith perceived reality, lived life, and consequently reflected and wrote of their experiences. The narrative of the Exodus from the land of Egypt, the foundational salvation story, images a strong and powerful savior God—at times even a warrior

God—who is victorious over Israel's enemies. At other times, Hebrew history reveals a God of blessing, a giver of all good gifts. This creation-rooted theology reveals a God of tenderness and care. Both theologies are sound biblical theologies, rooted in the scripture texts.[1]

However, with the coming of the horrors of modern warfare, many believers encounter the image of a warrior God as distant and uninviting. Others understand the warrior God in a somewhat different light, seeing this God as the one who overcomes evil, who stands on the side of the oppressed, whose justice overcomes the destructive forces in society over which they have no control.

To be sure, there are occasions when in our prayer we are drawn to implore the help of a God of power and strength. More often, however, we seek a personal God—one who knows us, a God who desires and invites our attentive presence and prayer. We are attracted to the compassionate and loving God, the God tenderly described by the prophet Isaiah (Isaiah 40:1–2; 43:1–4). We hear Jesus' invitation: "Come to me, all you that are weary and are carrying heavy burdens, and I will give you rest" (Matthew 11:28). Who is God for you? We can make no mistake if we seek the God of Jesus—the God of great love.

In modern times, we are privileged to receive a wealth of knowledge and insights unavailable to earlier generations. The work of biblical scholars over the past several decades helps us to better understand and appreciate the Word of God as living and active *today.* With expanded and deepened awareness, we gain new perspective that builds on what went before and opens up new vistas.

Research by scholars in the fields of biblical studies, theology, and spirituality sheds new light on our understanding of the social and cultural context of the New Testament: the place of women in the scriptures, their relationship to Jesus, their role in the faith community. Even the Hebrew scriptures (the First Testament) are rich with a wide range of images, texts, and names for the Holy One, references which have remained in the background far too long.

In the passages which follow, allow your personal experience, your way of experiencing and knowing, awaken you to the presence and the mystery of God in the here and now, God-for-me, God-for-us.

You will need a Bible to pray this chapter. For every scripture passage listed, you will find an introduction, an opening prayer, a guide for reflection, and a concluding prayer.

Each introduction offers a brief reflection on the selected verses with a particular focus on the theme of the prayer; for example, "God's personal love for me." The theme is not meant to limit the meaning of the text; the scriptures are rich and speak in various and diverse ways. The chosen focus, however, helps to offer you one helpful way to enter into the experience of praying the selected text.

The opening prayer begs the Holy Spirit for the grace to hear the sacred Word with the ears of my heart and to find in the text the message I am meant to hear.

The guide for reflection follows the reading of the scripture text. A few specific questions serve as a way of dialoging with the text—my experience in dialog with God's written Word, still alive and speaking to me today in my own circumstances.

In the concluding prayer, I draw my prayer to a close, giving thanks for the grace and gift of this time of communion with my God.

Once you become familiar with this way of praying with God's Word, choose your own favorite passages from the Bible and savor their richness as the texts speak to your heart.

Knowing God

God's Personal Love for Me: Isaiah 43:1–4

INTRODUCTION

This passage from the prophet Isaiah speaks of God's tender love for me, God's boundless interest and concern for me, and for all that concerns me. God's prophet spoke to my ancestors in the faith. God's living Word speaks to me today.

OPENING PRAYER

> Spirit of God, open the ears of my heart to hear and to understand your word to me today, a tender word of love and care.

READ THE SCRIPTURE PASSAGE

GUIDE FOR REFLECTION

- What speaks to my heart in these verses?
- Do I hear something today that I've not heard before? Or that I hear in a new way?
- What do the words tell me about how God loves? About God's relationship with me?
- How do these words speak to me at this time in my life?
- How is God inviting me to respond?
- Spend time with the One who loves you, and offer your love in return.

CONCLUDING PRAYER

Conclude your prayer with a few moments of silence; then in your own words give thanks for God's personal and enduring love. Some may feel called to express thanks in a non-verbal way—a bow, lifting one's hands to God, or some other gesture or song.

God's Intimate Knowledge of Me: Psalm 139:1–6, 13–17

INTRODUCTION

In this tender and touching reflection on God's intimate knowledge and infinite love for me, the sacred writer images God as a knitter, creating me in my mother's womb. God knows me from the moment of my conception. God knows each word I speak, each step I take.

OPENING PRAYER

> Spirit of God, pray in me. Awaken my heart to the gift of God's unique and unspeakable love for me, even from my mother's womb.

READ THE SCRIPTURE PASSAGE

GUIDE FOR REFLECTION

- Quiet your inner self, and be present to the God who loves you, who cradles you tenderly as a mother cradles the infant at her breast. Ask that you may hear and feel God's tender love.
- Then, slowly read aloud the words of the Psalm, pausing where a particular verse or image touches you.
- Be in touch with God's tender, motherly care for you, God's way of knowing you, even before you know yourself. Stay with this feeling, this revelation of God to you personally.

CONCLUDING PRAYER

Conclude your prayer by giving thanks to the God who so "fearfully and wonderfully" made you. Ask God to shape your own heart to love in this way—your own children and/or all with whom you are in relationship, all whose lives you touch and nurture.

Trust in God: Psalm 121

INTRODUCTION

Psalm 121 expresses trust in the Maker of heaven and earth, who upholds and protects me, never forgetting me, especially when I feel most vulnerable.

OPENING PRAYER

> God of my life, I come before you and pray for deep trust that you are always walking with me, are present to me, are carrying me in the most difficult times.

READ THE SCRIPTURE PASSAGE

GUIDE FOR REFLECTION

- No life is without its challenges, struggles, and crises. In the midst of dark, even stormy times, I feel my weakness and look about for support. Even as I draw on the strength of others, gradually I come to realize that what I most need is to reach deep within, to find my own inner strength, the presence of the Holy One, in-spiriting me, one-with-me.

- Name the worries that burden you at this time and ask the Holy One to pour healing balm onto your wounds. Repeat over and over your trust in God's care.

CONCLUDING PRAYER

Conclude your prayer by thanking the One who "keeps your life" and will never allow you to stumble. Place yourself in God's hands, and go in peace. Carry this prayer with you through the day: My help comes from my God, Maker of heaven and earth.

The Beauty of Creation: Psalm 19:1–4

INTRODUCTION

Psalm 19 gives heaven a voice to praise the glory of God! May we see with clear eyes the presence of the Creator who spread out the heavens and scooped out the mighty seas!

OPENING PRAYER

> Creating God, let me become more aware of your presence in the beauty of all that surrounds me—the expanse of the skies, the depth of the seas, the simple beauty of fields and flowers, however Nature clothes herself in this season.

READ THE SCRIPTURE PASSAGE

GUIDE FOR REFLECTION

- This is a perfect psalm to pray outdoors, if you like. Pause to savor God's artistry, the awesome signs of God's living presence. Pray the psalm slowly, let the words and images wash over you, and then let yourself be wrapped in the beauty of the rising morning sun, the evening sunset, or the starry night sky. Be aware of how nature speaks to you.

CONCLUDING PRAYER

Conclude with a simple expression of thanks for the beauty God provides for all our days, and resolve to do what you can today to care for the well-being of Earth.

Naomi and Ruth: A Faithful Relationship: Ruth 1:15–19

INTRODUCTION

The Book of Ruth narrates an engaging story of relationships and loyalty. Ruth is the Moabite widow (the "foreigner") who, faithful to her mother-in-law, Naomi (also a widow), departs Moab to journey back to Naomi's homeland of Judah (Bethlehem). Once they arrive in Bethlehem, Ruth's resourcefulness in preparing for life there depends on her developing new relationships. Treat yourself to a reading of the Book of Ruth (a four-chapter novella) to further appreciate and value this intelligent and wise "foreigner." Her marriage to Boaz brings her into the family line of Jesus—her son becomes the grandfather of David, the family line from which Jesus descends.

OPENING PRAYER

God of all nations, help me to glimpse in the story of these women your indiscriminate love for all the peoples of Earth. In Ruth and Naomi, let me see the value of relationships, of people caring for each other.

READ THE SCRIPTURE PASSAGE

GUIDE FOR REFLECTION

- In this inviting scripture passage, claim and celebrate the rich gifts of the women. Can you name situations in your own life where your own unique gifts turned misfortune into blessing? Reflect on your experiences.
- What strengths did you discover in yourself? Be in touch with the strengths God has given. Awake to the potential within you; call upon the indwelling Spirit of God, alive, active, and desirous of bringing you to fulfillment and deep inner joy.

CONCLUDING PRAYER

Conclude by giving thanks for the persons in your life who have been strong and faithful for you; give thanks that you have been given the grace to be strong and faithful for others.

The Desirability of Wisdom

Sophia: Holy Wisdom

INTRODUCTION

One of the images of God and one of the names of God from our Judeo-Christian heritage is *Sophia*, "Holy Wisdom." The passages below show the importance of Sophia in the Bible and the significance of her work.

OPENING PRAYER

Holy God, Sophia, open my heart to receive the light and wisdom you desire to give me. Free me, unlock whatever is closed in me, that I may be open to new ways of seeing what an amazing God you are!

> For she is a reflection of eternal light,
> a spotless mirror of the working of God,
> and an image of [God's] goodness.
> (Wisdom 7:26)
>
> She is easily discerned by those who love her,
> and is found by those who seek her.
> . . . she goes about seeking those worthy of her,
> . . . and meets them in every thought.
> (Wisdom 6:12, 16)

Therefore walk in the way of the good,
and keep to the paths of the just.
(Proverbs 2:20)

In every generation, she passes into holy souls
and makes them friends of God, and prophets. . . .
(Wisdom 7:27)

She is more beautiful than the sun,
and excels every constellation of the stars.
(Wisdom 7:29)

I was beside [God], like a master worker;
and I was daily his delight,
rejoicing before him always
rejoicing in his inhabited world
and delighting in the human race.
(Proverbs 8:30–31)

GUIDE FOR REFLECTION

- Read each of the above verses reflectively. Which one(s) speak to you in a special way? Can you recall God as Sophia, Holy Wisdom, present to you in some specific life experience (e.g., joy, challenge, difficulty, decision)?
- In your own prayer and reflection, can you identify with this expression/name of God as Holy Wisdom? As you reflect on your own daily living, are there moments or times when you are aware of God in this way—as being present to you, as being "with-you"?
- In your own words, in your own style, speak to this loving God, Holy Wisdom, Divine Presence.

CONCLUDING PRAYER

Conclude by thanking God, who continues to reveal in our own lifetimes in fresh and often unexpected ways.

Mary

Mary: the Traveling Disciple

INTRODUCTION

When we think about it, how often have our "pictures" of Mary been shaped by holy cards or statues in our parish churches? While these offer tender images, other lively and refreshing word-pictures of Mary exist in the gospels. Have you ever stopped to notice how much traveling Mary does as her life unfolds? Mary's life in the scriptures is dramatically framed by the Spirit's presence—the Annunciation: "The Holy Spirit will come upon you"; and Pentecost: the descent of the Spirit upon the praying believers in the upper room. Truly, Mary is a woman with a remarkable life journey, a journey suffused with the life of the Spirit!

Mary's first journey is prompted by Gabriel's news that her cousin Elizabeth is to have a child. Then "with haste," Mary travels into the hill country of Judea to stay at her cousin's home. After the birth of Elizabeth's son, John, Mary returns to Nazareth. What follows is the trip to Bethlehem with Joseph for the census. Anxiously, the family makes a hurried flight into Egypt. In due time, they return to Galilee; the family travels in a caravan to Jerusalem to celebrate Passover, and we read of the Child Jesus lost in the Temple.

Later, we find Mary at Cana for the wedding feast, speaking up so that the guests will have more wine! She shows up in a crowded scene during Jesus' itinerant preaching ministry. Tradition tells us she met him on the Via Dolorosa, the way of the cross. Finally, heartbroken, she stands at the foot of the cross.

After the Resurrection, we find her in Jerusalem with the apostles, no doubt praying with them and pondering the meaning of all that had happened. After Jesus' Ascension, the Holy Spirit explodes into their prayer (Pentecost) while they huddle in the upper room.

GUIDE FOR REFLECTION

Select one of the passages below, and imagine yourself as Mary's traveling companion. Engage in conversation with her, heart-to-heart. What may be her concerns about this trip? Do you have any experiences that help you to identify with her? Share these with Mary, truly your sister, your mother.

Mary visits Elizabeth	Luke 1:39–56
Mary travels to Bethlehem	Luke 2:1–7
Mary travels to Jerusalem (The Purification)	Luke 2:22–24

Mary flees to Egypt with Joseph and the Christ Child	Matthew 2:13–15
The Holy Family returns to Galilee	Luke 2:39–40
The Holy Family travels to Jerusalem for Passover	Luke 2:41–52
Mary travels to Cana for the wedding feast	John 2:1–11
Pentecost	Acts 1:12–2:4

CONCLUDING PRAYER

Conclude by asking for that total openness to the Spirit which marked Mary's life journey. And give thanks that an ordinary woman like Mary can be your companion, your sister, your mother.

Mary Visits Elizabeth: Luke 1:39–56

INTRODUCTION

The Visitation narrative presents a powerful scene from the Gospel of Luke—so much so that it invites further reflection. What a marvelous icon we have in the encounter of these two pregnant women. Cousins from different generations, the elder Elizabeth looks into the face of the youthful Mary and recognizes God's blessing, God's visitation on both of them. Elizabeth exultantly cries out that the infant stirred in her womb at the sound of Mary's voice.

And it is Elizabeth's joy, as she names God's action in their lives, which frees Mary to sing out: "My soul proclaims the greatness of the Lord."

OPENING PRAYER

> Wise Elizabeth, eager Mary, may your shared joy spill over into my heart. Touched by your joy, may I awaken to the ways God takes flesh in my own life journey.

GUIDE FOR REFLECTION

Find a quiet spot, open your Bible to this passage, and enter the text as though for the first time. Read it slowly, reverently. Imagine you are there . . . perhaps as a young neighbor from the village, helping Elizabeth, privileged to observe these two women. Notice, it is "the elder pregnant woman who becomes midwife to the Word. She hears Mary into speech," and points to this "extraordinary, explosive moment of insight" as the first prophetic utterance of the New Testament.[2]

Who are the ones who have helped you to see Christ being born in your life? Recall the wisdom shared by those who have gone before you. Give thanks for their presence in your life. How have you helped others to see Christ being born in their life situations?

CONCLUDING PRAYER

Conclude by thanking Mary and Elizabeth for their privileged place in the story of salvation, or you may use this prayer from one of the early mystics:

> Blessed are you, Mary! You constantly felt the body of Christ, created from your own body, grow and move in your womb until the time of his birth. You touched him, wrapped him in clothes, laid him in a manger and nursed and nurtured him. . . . Blessed are you, holy Mary![3]

Mary's Hymn of Praise (The Magnificat): *Luke* 1:46–55

INTRODUCTION

Mary's hymn, the first canticle of Luke's gospel, sounds a chorus of praise for the God who does great things! Prophetically, her insight into how *God sees* and the way *God acts* in relationship to all peoples offers a first glimpse of the new order that Jesus will proclaim in word and in deed. Jesus' preaching and action turn the existing order on its head. Jesus' love for the poor and the marginalized incarnates God's inclusive love for all peoples. (Hannah's prayer in 1 Samuel 2:1–10 serves as a model for Mary's hymn of praise in Luke's gospel).

OPENING PRAYER

> Mary, woman of faith, my companion, my mother, share with me your deep faith in God's plan. Help me to say "yes" and to trust the wisdom of God's ways.

READ THE SCRIPTURE PASSAGE

GUIDE FOR REFLECTION

As you open your Bible to this passage, enter the text as though for the first time. Read it slowly, reverently. Imagine you are there . . . and hear Mary's words. In a world where poverty, violation of human rights, the abuse and exclusion of women cry out for justice, we recognize the timelessness of Mary's prayer. Then, reflect for a few moments on an image of suffering from the recent news—in your own community or beyond.

Touched by the pain of sisters and brothers in need, pour out your concerns for them. Beg God to tenderly uphold and enfold them with gentle love.

CONCLUDING PRAYER

Conclude by praying again Mary's canticle. You may choose to use the following translation of Mary's Song.

> Sing out my soul,
> sing of the holiness of God:
> who has delighted in a woman,
> lifted up the poor,
> satisfied the hungry,
> given voice to the silent,
> grounded the oppressor,
> blessed the full-bellied
> with emptiness,
> and with the gift of tears
> those who have never wept:
> who has desired the darkness
> of the womb,
> and inhabited our flesh.
> Sing of the longing of God,
> sing out, my soul.[4]

> *Mantra* to carry with you throughout the day: God, who is mighty, has done great things for me! Holy is God's name!

Jesus and Women

One of the striking features of the ministry of Jesus in the gospels is his attention to those on society's margins—the poor, the diseased, tax collectors, those not of his religious heritage, children, and women—to name but a few. In the society and culture of Palestine and its environs, women simply didn't count. Yet we find numerous examples throughout Jesus' public ministry where he reached out to women, brought them into his inner circle, *noticed* them, entered into conversation with them. Jesus engaged with the Samaritan woman at the well; the Canaanite woman seeking a cure for her daughter; the woman who touched his cloak seeking a cure; and those who followed him and ministered to him throughout his travels, especially Martha and Mary and Mary Magdalene, who were his close friends. As we come to understand more clearly the meaning of the gospels, and as we allow the gospel characters to become more than "holy card images"—rather living, three-dimensional personalities, we begin to discover that Jesus, too, was a vibrant, engaged human person, revealing the inclusive love of God for every member of the human family. In the following passages, note the outreach, the interest, the compassion of Jesus in his relationship with a variety of women in diverse circumstances.

Jairus's Daughter and the Woman with the Issue of Blood: Mark 5:25–34

INTRODUCTION

Two stories intertwine here: a twelve-year-old girl near death, who is the daughter of Jairus, a synagogue official; and the unnamed woman who for twelve years has been suffering with the issue of blood. Because of her illness, she has been separated and isolated from both the religious community and society. Having no one to speak for her, she reaches out to touch Jesus, and thus initiates her own cure.

How astounding that in our sacred texts, we find this earthy story! Every woman knows this monthly cycle of discomfort, oftentimes pain, weakness, and even emotional fragility. And what strength! In faith (and desperation?) she reaches out for relief, for healing. At once, she feels she is whole again. Simultaneously, Jesus feels that power has gone out from him. Not a word, only touch. How very much like the instincts we feel in the presence of suffering—to hold the sick child, to take the hand of the one who is bedridden, to wipe the brow, to kiss the scraped knee.

OPENING PRAYER

> Jesus, compassion of God, in this prayer, may I reach out in faith to touch you and be healed of all that keeps me from the wholeness and peace that I long for.

READ THE SCRIPTURE PASSAGE

GUIDE FOR REFLECTION

- Take the place of the woman who touches Jesus. What does it feel like to summon up the faith, the confidence that you will be made whole, that your brokenness will be healed? That all your past efforts will not be in vain? You have done all that you could, and now you are in the hands of the Holy One.

- Take the place of Jesus, who experiences that "power has gone out from him." Recall experiences where your touch, your words brought peace, brought healing.

CONCLUDING PRAYER

Conclude by giving thanks to God whose compassion and power are revealed again in the lives of those who trust him.

The Woman Who Anointed Jesus: Mark 14:3–9

INTRODUCTION

What a marvelous story here, where an unnamed woman takes center stage at a dinner party hosted by Simon. The details of the party fade; though the host is named, nothing more is made of him.

The central action belongs to the unnamed woman. Perhaps she was one of the servant maids. We know her only as the one who extravagantly anoints the head of Jesus (as Christ, as Messiah) with costly perfume. The guests criticize her for such waste: "This ointment could have been sold . . . and the money given to the poor."

But Jesus, on the threshold of his Passion, sees more. He understands her action as preparation for his burial. His praise of her echoes, though silently, through the years: "Wherever the good news is proclaimed in the whole world, what she has done will be told in memory of her."

OPENING PRAYER

> Jesus, I pray for the freedom to respond to the needs of the moment with a spontaneous and generous—even outrageous—offering of self.

READ THE SCRIPTURE PASSAGE

GUIDE FOR REFLECTION

- As you reflect on this passage, accompany this unnamed woman to that banquet scene. Assist her in the anointing, and hear Jesus' praise. Her extravagance stands in bold relief, preceded and followed with verses about Jesus' betrayal, and the chief priests' offer to Judas—money—if he will hand Jesus over.
- She may not have been able to save Jesus; she may not have been able to speak up in his defense, but Jesus recognizes that "she did what she could."
- Reflect on your own life circumstances, your response to situations of need, of request. At times, it is not within our power to "fix" or radically change things. Often, our response is to do what we can, and to pray that our efforts will be like healing ointment, that our action will be received as a loving gesture of compassion.

CONCLUDING PRAYER

Conclude by giving thanks for the awareness to be able to respond with your gifts, your energies, your insights. Pray for the grace to be generous and to see those places in your world where love can be a healing balm.

The Bent-Over Woman: Luke 13:10–13

INTRODUCTION

The bent-over woman: what a marvelous icon of human nature, weighed down by the trials, demands, and burdens of life. As Jesus teaches in the synagogue on the Sabbath, "there appeared a woman with a spirit that had crippled her for eighteen years." Unnamed, described only by her infirmity, Jesus notices her, calls her over, and utters the healing words, "Woman, you are set free from your ailment."

How often are we like the bent-over woman! Perhaps not physically, but in spirit: dragged down, depressed, no spirited life within. Daily routine, the difficulties of a job, strain in relationships, financial drain, serious illness—whether our own or that of a family member or a dear friend—pending death of a loved one, diminishment . . .

Burdened, I come before Jesus, healer and friend. Mindful of my own needs, I am confident of his love and compassion.

OPENING PRAYER

> Jesus, healer and friend, help me to name what keeps me bent over, and call me to stand tall before you. I trust your power to make me whole.

READ THE SCRIPTURE PASSAGE

GUIDE FOR REFLECTION

- Ask yourself: What is keeping me from standing tall, being all that I can be? What burdens my heart? What is dragging me down? Picture yourself in the presence of Jesus, and hear him say—"Woman, you are set free from your ailment."
- It is the compassionate Jesus who addresses me: "Let me carry the burden with you, so that you may stand tall. See, I place my Spirit within you; you are not alone." Let these words seep into your heart and bring healing.
- Or, you may wish to speak with this gospel woman who now stands tall, free, healed! Let her describe to you her experience. Finally, the long years of suffering are past, and she begins a new life. Imagine what that may be like for her—and for you.

CONCLUDING PRAYER

Conclude by speaking your trust in the One who lifts you up. Or, you may wish to savor these words from Psalm 57:

> Be merciful to me, O God, be merciful to me,
> for in you my soul takes refuge;
> in the shadow of your wings I will take refuge,
> until the destroying storms pass by. . . .
>
> Awake, O harp and lyre!
> I will awake the dawn.

I will give thanks to you, O Lord, among the peoples...
For your steadfast love is as high as the heavens;
your faithfulness extends to the clouds.

The Canaanite Woman: Matthew 15:21–28

INTRODUCTION

Of all the encounters between Jesus and women in the gospels, there is a unique and startling quality about this unnamed woman, marginalized, an "outsider" from Canaan. She appeals to Jesus, calls him, "Lord" and begs for the cure of her daughter. Her concern is not for herself, but for her daughter—another gospel woman defined by relationship.

Curiously, Jesus initially dismisses her request and then grants it. Does the Canaanite woman change Jesus' mind? The compelling dialog seems to suggest such. First he ignores her cry; then the apostles, quite annoyed, ask him to send her away. But she persists, and Jesus' next words startle us: "It is not fair to take the children's food and throw it to the dogs." Cleverly, she takes Jesus' image of the dogs and turns it to her advantage—"Yes, Lord, yet even the dogs eat the crumbs that fall from their masters' table."

Note this woman's fierce determination to be heard. Though not a member of "the chosen," she brings a deep faith in

Jesus' power. And neither the impatience of the apostles nor the rebuff of Jesus deters her. She claims her place and insists on being heard. The one she acknowledges as "Lord" cannot resist—Jesus grants her request and accords her the highest praise: "Woman, great is your faith!" We can't help but admire her dogged persistence, her insistence on being heard.

OPENING PRAYER

> Jesus, you came to herald a new order. Open my eyes that I may learn from you to reach beyond common expectations and established conventions when I hear the cry of a sister or brother in need. Give me the courage to speak up, to act when basic human needs are being overlooked or ignored.

READ THE SCRIPTURE PASSAGE

GUIDE FOR REFLECTION

- Reflect on Jesus in this gospel setting. Are there situations in your world, in your local area where speaking out requires courage? Reflect on your circumstances. Are you bound and hemmed in by conventions or by the status quo or popular opinion? Do you need to raise questions or press for a change?
- Be encouraged by this Canaanite gospel sister, and pray for insight and wisdom, for courage to speak.

CONCLUDING PRAYER

Conclude by giving thanks to the One who places within you all the power that you need. Pray that God give you the strength to claim that grace.

Jesus' Comforting Care for Us: Matthew 11:28ff

INTRODUCTION

These tender words of Jesus are words we often return to for comfort and consolation. Scripture scholars tell us that Jesus is described here with the qualities given in the Wisdom tradition. As the incarnation of Holy Wisdom, Sophia, Jesus embodies a special relationship to all of creation, especially to those who suffer. Jesus is the compassion of God; Jesus shows us the face of God. At one point, Jesus wept over Jerusalem (who refused his invitation). He compares himself to a mother hen who gathers her chicks under her wing.

OPENING PRAYER

> Jesus, you call me to come to you, especially when I am troubled and sad. Be present to me now, for I seek the consolation and the tender love, which you have promised to those who turn to you.

READ THE SCRIPTURE PASSAGE

GUIDE FOR REFLECTION

Consider this reflection of Anselm of Canterbury, or speak to Jesus in your own words, laying your burdens before him. Hear his words of comfort, and give thanks.

> But you, too, good Jesus, are you not also a
> mother?
> Are you not a mother who, like a hen, gathers
> her chicks beneath her wings?. . .
> And you, my soul, dead in yourself,
> run under the wings of Jesus your mother
> and lament your griefs under his feathers.
> Ask that your wounds may be healed
> and that, comforted, you may live again.
>
> Christ, my mother,
> you gather your chickens under your wings;
> This dead chicken of yours puts [her]self under
> those wings . . .
> Warm your chicken, give life to your dead [one],
> justify your inner.[5]

CONCLUDING PRAYER

Conclude your prayer by spending a few moments in silence with Jesus, the motherly and comforting One.

Mary Magdalene Meets the Risen Christ: John 20:11, 15–18

INTRODUCTION

We have become accustomed to a "blended" story of the resurrection appearances, in which the various accounts of the different gospel writers are stitched together into one narrative. In doing this, we lose the startling revelation of this passage from John's gospel. In John, Mary is the first *to witness* the risen Jesus, and then the first *to tell* the resurrection story. An early Christian writer named her "apostle to the apostles." Don't miss the startling and unique role given to this woman, this faithful disciple of Jesus. Her fidelity, her hope, her great love still speak to us centuries later.

OPENING PRAYER

> Risen One, I thank you for the gift of faith, and I pray that my faith be enlivened and strengthened by your grace. Help me to live in the new reality of a world transformed by you.

READ THE SCRIPTURE PASSAGE

GUIDE FOR REFLECTION

- With Mary, look upon the face of the living Christ, and claim him as your "Rabbouni," your teacher.
- Where is the risen One present in your life? In the lives of those who intersect with yours? In the places where there is non-life (apathy, discouragement, despair), how am I called

to bring life? How am I called to witness to life in the places where I am sent?

CONCLUDING PRAYER

Conclude your prayer by praying for the light to know your call; pray for those women in your life who strengthen and enliven your own faith. Give thanks for them.

CHAPTER SIX

Prayers from the Tradition

These familiar prayers come from our Catholic Christian treasury. Many we learned as children, in the home or in religion classes. In a few instances, the language has been updated so that it flows more smoothly. These spoken prayer texts can become the subject of reflective prayer.

Reflecting on or praying the Lord's Prayer, for example, means we somehow "inhabit" the prayer; we enter into a deeper communion with the One who gives us each day our daily bread. We "unpack" the phrases. For example, what is daily bread for me? What do I need to be nourished, to be fed? Reflecting on the words of the familiar prayer texts, we are at a place where the words become personal to me; I somehow "own" them. Then, when I pray the Lord's Prayer at the Eucharist, or in another setting, those sentiments of trust in God's providence well up in me. I am saying more than just words. My heart has been touched; I own the prayer in a new way.

So it is and will be for any of the prayer texts in this section when we spend time getting inside the meaning and linking our own desires with the words of the spoken prayer.

In truth, when we have pondered and "prayed" the texts, our spoken prayer is enriched.

Classic Christian Prayers

The Lord's Prayer

Our Father, who art in heaven, hallowed be thy name.
Thy kingdom come, thy will be done
on earth as it is in heaven.
Give us this day our daily bread
and forgive us our trespasses
as we forgive those who trespass against us.
And lead us not into temptation,
but deliver us from evil.
Amen.

The Hail Mary

Hail Mary, full of grace!
The Lord is with thee.
Blessed art thou among women,

and blessed is the fruit of thy womb, Jesus.
Holy Mary, Mother of God,
pray for us sinners,
now and at the hour of our death.
Amen.

The Glory Be (the "doxology," a word of praise)

Glory be to the Father,
and to the Son
and to the Holy Spirit!
As it was in the beginning,
is now and ever shall be,
world without end.
Amen.

Sometimes you will see this contemporary translation.

Glory to the Father and to the Son,
and to the Holy Spirit!
As it was in the beginning, is now,
and will be forever. Amen.

The Apostles' Creed

I believe in God, the Father Almighty,
Creator of heaven and earth;
and in Jesus Christ, his only Son, our Lord,
who was conceived by the Holy Spirit,
born of the Virgin Mary,

suffered under Pontius Pilate,
was crucified, died and was buried.
He descended into hell,
the third day rose again from the dead.
He ascended into heaven
and is seated at the right hand of the Father.
He will come again to judge the living and the dead.
I believe in the Holy Spirit,
the holy catholic church, the communion of saints,
the forgiveness of sins,
the resurrection of the body,
and life everlasting. Amen.

The Confiteor

I confess to almighty God,
and to you, my brothers and sisters,
that I have sinned through my own fault
in my thoughts and in my words,
in what I have done ,
and in what I have failed to do;
and I ask blessed Mary, ever virgin,
all the angels and saints,
and you, my bothers and sisters,
to pray for me to the Lord our God.

A Short Act of Faith, Hope, Love

Jesus, I believe in you.
Jesus, I hope in you.
Jesus, I love you.

Act of Faith

O God,
I firmly believe all the truths that you have revealed,
and that you teach us through your Church,
for you are truth itself
and can neither deceive nor be deceived.[1]

Act of Hope (traditional wording)

O my God, relying on your infinite goodness and promises,
I hope to obtain pardon of my sins,
the help of your grace,
and life everlasting,
through the merits of Jesus Christ, my Lord and Redeemer.[2]

Act of Hope (a contemporary text)

O God,
I hope with complete trust that you will give me,
through the merits of Jesus Christ,
all necessary grace in this world
and everlasting life in the world to come,
for this is what you have promised
and you always keep your promises.

Act of Love

O God,
I love you with my whole heart above all things,
because you are infinitely good;
and for your sake I love my neighbor as I love myself.[3]

Act of Sorrow (Contrition)

O God,
I am sorry with my whole heart for all my sins
because you are Goodness itself
and sin is an offense against you.
Therefore, I firmly resolve,
with the help of your grace,
not to sin again and to avoid the occasions of sin.

Act of Sorrow (from St. Alphonsus Liguori)

I love you, Jesus, my love.
I love you with all my heart.
I repent of having offended you.
Never permit me to offend you again.
Grant that I may love you always,
and then do with me what you will.
Amen.[4]

Act of Sorrow (from Luke 18:13)

God, be merciful to me, a sinner!

Prayer to the Holy Spirit

Come, Holy Spirit!
Fill the hearts of your faithful
and kindle in them the fire of your love.
Send forth your spirit, and they shall be created
and you will renew the face of the earth.

Lord, by the light of the Holy Spirit,
you have enlightened the hearts of your faithful.
In the same Spirit,
may we come to relish what is right
and always rejoice in your consolation.
We ask this through Christ our Lord.
Amen.

Mysteries of the Rosary

The Joyful Mysteries

1. The Annunciation
2. The Visitation
3. The Nativity
4. The Presentation in the Temple
5. The Finding in the Temple

The Luminous Mysteries/Mysteries of Light

1. The Baptism of our Lord in the Jordan
2. The Wedding at Cana
3. The Proclamation of the Kingdom of God
4. The Transfiguration
5. The Institution of the Eucharist

The Sorrowful Mysteries

1. The Agony in the Garden
2. The Scourging at the Pillar
3. The Crowning with Thorns
4. Jesus Carries his Cross
5. The Crucifixion

The Glorious Mysteries

1. The Resurrection
2. The Ascension
3. The Descent of the Holy Spirit
4. The Assumption of Our Lady
5. The Crowning of Our Lady

The Angelus

This prayer recalls the Incarnation: God's eternal Word entering human history. Christians traditionally paused to pray this prayer when they heard the church bells toll at six o'clock in the morning, at noon, and again at six o'clock in the evening.

The angel of the Lord declared unto Mary,
and she conceived by the Holy Spirit.
Hail Mary . . .

Behold the handmaid of the Lord;
be it done to me according to thy word.

Hail Mary . . .

And the Word was made flesh;
and dwelled among us.

Hail Mary . . .
Pray for us, O Holy Mother of God,
that we may be made worthy of the promises of Christ.

Let us pray:
Pour forth, we beseech thee, O Lord,
Thy grace into our hearts,
that we to whom the Incarnation of Christ, thy Son,
was made known by the message of an angel,
may, by his passion and cross,
be brought to the glory of his resurrection,
through the same Christ our Lord.
Amen.

Regina Coeli (Latin, "Queen of Heaven")

Prayed during the Easter season, in place of the Angelus.

O, Queen of Heaven, rejoice!
Alleluia.
For He whom you did merit to bear,
Alleluia,

Has arisen as He said,
Alleluia.
Pray for us to God,
Alleluia.
Rejoice and be glad, O Virgin Mary.
Alleluia.
For Our Lord has risen indeed.
Alleluia.
Let us pray.
O God, who, through the Resurrection of your Son our Lord Jesus Christ,
willed to fill the world with joy;
grant, that, through His Virgin Mother, Mary,
we may lay hold on the joys of everlasting life
through the same Christ our Lord. Amen.

The Gospel Canticles

The Gospel Canticles are often referred to as "mini-gospels"—praising God for the gift of our salvation in Jesus Christ. As we begin the prayer, we sign ourselves with the cross, the traditional mark of Christ's saving death and resurrection.

Canticle of Zachary, (The Benedictus)

Prayed in the morning.

Blessed are you, Lord God of Israel,
you have come to your people and set them free.
You have raised up for us a mighty Savior,
born of the house of your servant David.
Through your holy prophets, you promised of old
    to save us from our enemies,

from the hands of all who hate us,
to show mercy to our forebears,
and to remember your holy covenant.
This was the oath God swore to our father Abraham:
to set us free from the hands of our enemies,
free to worship you without fear,
holy and righteous before you,
all the days of our life.
And you, child, shall be called the prophet of the Most High,
for you will go before the Lord to prepare the way,
to give God's people the knowledge of salvation
by the forgiveness of their sins.
In the tender compassion of our God
the dawn from on high shall break upon us,
to shine on those who dwell in darkness and the shadow of death,
and to guide our feet into the way of peace.

Canticle of Mary (The Magnificat)

Prayed in the evening.

My soul proclaims the greatness of the Lord,
my spirit rejoices in God my Savior,
for you, Lord, have looked with favor on your lowly servant.
From this day all generations will call me blessed:
you, the Almighty, have done great things for me
and holy is your name.
You have mercy on those who fear you,
from generation to generation.

You have shown strength with your arm
and scattered the proud in their conceit,
casting down the mighty from their thrones,
and lifting up the lowly.
You have filled the hungry with good things
and sent the rich away empty.
You have come to the aid of your servant Israel,
to remember the promise of mercy,
the promise made to our forebears,
to Abraham and his children for ever.

Canticle of Simeon (The Nunc Dimittis)

Prayed at night.

Now, Lord, you let your servant go in peace;
your word has been fulfilled:
my own eyes have seen the salvation
which you have prepared in the sight of every people:
a light to reveal you to the nations
and the glory of your people Israel.

Memorare to Our Lady

Remember, O most gracious Virgin Mary
that never was it known,
that anyone who fled to your protection,
implored your help, or sought your intercession
was left unaided.
Inspired by this confidence, we fly unto you,
O Virgin of virgins, our Mother!

To you we come, before you we stand,
sinful and sorrowful.
O Mother of the Word incarnate,
despise not our petitions,
but in your mercy hear and answer me.
Amen.

Stations of the Cross

We adore you, O Christ and we bless you,
because by your holy cross, you have redeemed the world.

1. Jesus is condemned to death.
2. Jesus accepts his cross.
3. Jesus falls the first time.
4. Jesus meets his mother.
5. Simon helps Jesus carry the cross.
6. Veronica wipes the face of Jesus.
7. Jesus falls the second time.
8. Jesus speaks to the women of Jerusalem.
9. Jesus falls the third time.
10. Jesus is stripped of his garments.
11. Jesus is nailed to the cross.
12. Jesus dies on the cross.
13. Jesus is taken down from the cross.
14. Jesus is laid in the tomb.

Take, Lord, Receive (The Suscipe)

Take, O Lord, into your hands,
my entire liberty,
my memory,
my understanding
and my will.
All that I am and have,
you have given me,
and I surrender them to you
to be disposed of
according to your will.
Give me your love and your grace;
with these I am rich enough
and desire nothing more.[5]

Lord, I Freely Yield (The Suscipe, a contemporary translation)

Lord, I freely yield all my freedom to you.
Take my memory, my intellect and my entire will.
You have given me everything I am or have;
I give it all back to you to stand under your will alone.
Your love and your grace are enough for me;
I shall ask for nothing more.[6]

Prayer to One's Guardian Angel

Angel of God, my guardian dear,
to whom God's love commits me here.
Ever this day be at my side,

to light and guard,
to rule and guide.
Amen.

St. Francis of Assisi's Prayer for Peace

Lord, make me an instrument of your peace.
Where there is hatred, let me sow love;
Where there is injury, pardon;
Where there is doubt, faith;
Where there is despair, hope;
Where there is darkness, light;
Where there is sadness, joy.
O Divine Master,
let me not so much seek to be consoled
as to console;
to be understood, as to understand;
to be loved, as to love.
For it is in giving that we receive.
It is in pardoning that we are pardoned;
it is in dying that we are born to eternal life.

Words That Invite Reflection

From Sacred Scripture

Many of the reflections below come either directly from scripture or are deeply influenced by scriptural texts. These short verses give expression to feelings of the heart—faith, sorrow, acceptance, trust, love, etc. I can carry the prayer with me through the day, a simple way of being in touch with God.

Lord, that I may see!

I do believe; help my unbelief!

O God, be merciful, to me a sinner.

Be it done to me according to your word.

Into your hands I commend my spirit.

Lord, I am not worthy that you should come under my roof.

Speak, Lord, your servant is listening.

My God, my God, why have you forsaken me?

Lord, to whom shall we go? You have the words of everlasting life.

Your word, Lord, is spirit and truth.

Your word is a lamp for my feet and a light to my path.

The Lord is my shepherd; I shall not want.

You are the Christ, the Son of the Living God!

Show us the Father, and it is enough for us.

My Lord and my God!

Bless the Lord, my soul; and all my being praise God's holy name!

As a deer longs for flowing streams, so my soul longs for you, O God.

My soul proclaims the greatness of the Lord; my spirit rejoices in God my savior.

Hear my prayer, O Lord; let my cry come to you.

Bless the Lord, O my soul, and all that is within me, bless his holy name.

To you, O Lord, I lift up my soul. O my God, in you I trust.

Be merciful to me, O God, be merciful to me, for in you, my soul takes refuge.

Let the peoples praise you, O God; let all the peoples praise you.

O sing to the Lord a new song; sing to the Lord, all the earth.

What shall I return to the Lord for all God's bounty to me?

PART THREE

An Invitation to Pray Together

Our Christian tradition is rich in rituals for common prayer—the celebration of Eucharist and all the sacraments, prayer at the beginning and ending of the day, prayer that marks the seasons of the Church year. More than words, ritual prayer is a rhythm of sound and silence, stillness and movement, song and spoken word, symbols that speak to our senses and evoke the Holy Mystery that pulses through all of life, all of creation. The richness of ritual language reveals itself to us when we pause . . . and take a long, loving look.

Think of these sacred signs as windows that invite our gaze to *see* (experience) the presence of the Holy. The Mystery at the heart is clothed in what our eyes see, our ears hear, our hands touch. "Taste and see the goodness of the Lord" (Psalm 34:8).

Celtic spirituality speaks of "the thin places," those times, objects, experiences where the presence of God breaks into our very ordinary life-routines. Thus there is a prayer for kindling the fire, for baking the bread, for tilling the earth, for spring planting, etc. The liturgy, too, is meant to be that unique "thin place" where the mystery of God's presence breaks through, where we recognize in word and gesture, in silence and song the Holy in our midst.

One noted Catholic writer put it this way:

> Catholics live in an enchanted world, a world of statues and holy water, stained glass and votive candles, saints and religious medals, rosary beads and holy pictures. But these Catholic paraphernalia are mere hints of a deeper and more pervasive religious sensibility which includes Catholics who see the Holy lurking in creation. As Catholics, we find our houses and our world haunted by a sense that the objects, events, and persons of daily life are revelations of grace.[1]

"An Invitation to Pray Together" includes chapters on liturgy, with special attention paid to reflections on selected gestures, words, objects; prayer at set times of the day: morning, midday, evening, night; and the Church's feasts and seasons: Advent, Christmastide, Lent, Triduum, Easter, and Pentecost.

CHAPTER SEVEN

Gestures, Words, and Objects

The texts that follow invite reflection on selected elements of the liturgy. Attending to these familiar words, gestures, and objects can reveal the presence of God, the holy clothed in the ordinary. Upon closer reflection, these simple elements offer a window into the mystery present at the heart of our liturgical prayer. Choose one of the passages below. As you reflect on its meaning, ask that you may grow in awareness and attentiveness to this part of the liturgy.

Liturgical Prayers and Reflections

Sign of the Cross

Begin this prayer by slowly, reverently making the Sign of the Cross. This is the universal sign that marks us as Christians, followers of Jesus Christ, who in his passion, death, and resurrection showed us the way to life.

At the beginning and end of this Mass;
at the beginning and end of our lives;
at the beginning and ending of all we do
stands the sign of the cross, saying:
this place, this space of time, this life,
this child, these people, this corpse,
belongs to the Lord and will not be
snatched from Him
who bears indelibly in His body
the marks of that same cross.[1]

Conclude your reflection by recalling a few instances in your life when the Sign of the Cross was especially meaningful to you. Give thanks for the life, death, and resurrection of Jesus. As you make the Sign of the Cross, re-claim this universal Christian sign as your own sign that life will always triumph over death.

Let Us Pray

How often have I heard this familiar invitation! After hearing the words "let us pray," how do I quiet my mind and open my heart to welcome the Spirit, who prays within me? How can this invitation help me to pray now?

> An invitation
> to still our gathered selves,
> a quiet pause
> to open up space
> where each may stand in the Presence
> filled with praise and wonder,
> pondering within
> together:
> echoing,
> swelling,
> spilling over,
> caught up and embraced in word and gesture
> by one gifted
> to speak aloud
> the prayer voiced
> in the silence of each heart.[2]

> Thank you, my God, for the invitation and the grace to turn to you. During the coming day, remind me of how easy it is to turn to you in a few simple words of prayer.

Do This in Memory

In memory of Jesus, I come together with others to draw strength for living a life of loving and giving. I pray to say "no" to the death in me; to shout "yes!" to the life in me. The Eucharist is ever linked with my daily life.

Pausing to say good-bye
a motley crew gathered
to share a final meal
to break bread
to remember
the long roads walked side by side
the crowds fed miraculously, but simply
the dark storms endured
the Word that had lived in flesh among them
the life they had given so
that others might also know
a love that touched and transformed
the fearful into a body of bold believers.
Pausing to remember
we still come together
a broken and searching people
to retell our Lord's stories
to defeat death
by the power of this communion
by remembering.[3]

Loving Jesus, give me a renewed and deepened awareness that when I share the table of the Eucharist with others, I find you there with us. I come to know you in the breaking of the breed, as did the disciples at Emmaus.

Go in Peace

"The gift that you have received, give as a gift." Think back to a recent celebration of the Eucharist. Recall your "frame of mind" when you entered the church, when the celebration began. Recall your feelings as the celebration ended, and you heard the words, "Go in peace." Were you given a special grace? Were your spirits lifted up? Give thanks to the Giver of all gifts. Ask yourself: "What gift have I been given that I can share this week?"

Go in the peace of Christ . . .
However we came
however confused or discouraged
          or afraid or alone
we may have been
before this Eucharist
we are told to leave in peace.
Presumably something has happened here:
We have found direction and courage
dispelled fear
been in communion,
thereby discovering the peace of Christ.
"Thanks be to God."

The Mass is ended: Go in peace . . .
However tenuously,
however unconsciously,
however fleetingly,
we have been changed

in the actions of this Eucharist,
in coming together,
submitting to God's Word
and sharing his table,
therein learning the peace of Christ.
"Thanks be to God."

Go in peace to love and serve the Lord . . .
However complicated
however full of suffering
however plain and ordinary
our everyday lives
we are told now to return there
knowing what the Lord has done for us
and what he commissions us to do:
"The dawn from on high has broken upon us
and has set our feet
in the path of peace."
"Thanks be to God."[4]

Recall last Sunday's celebration of the Eucharist, the grace or awareness that you received. Pray that you may "live that grace" in your day-to-day living.

Altar Table

I look upon this table—large or small, simple or ornate—it is my family table. It gathers us all; it is where I belong; here I am at home.

Banquet table
table of the Lord
table of the Lord's people
open to all, ready for all
Jew/Greek
slave/free
male/female
Come, sit at the "welcome table"
free seating for all
no reserved seats
no partiality
no discrimination.
"You are all one in Christ Jesus." (Galatians 3)[5]

During Jesus' life on earth, the table was a unique gathering place, a place of special ministry open to all. Pray to live this mystery of Christ's inclusive, welcoming love at all the tables or gathering places where you meet his brothers and sisters.

Cup and Plate

Have I ever thought of myself as a holy vessel, shaped of a unique design, color, and purpose to bear Christ to others? Have I ever reflected that I am a living sacrament—created by God to make God's love visible to the world?

Chalice cup and paten
fashioned from earth's core
fire-tried
molded
shaped for sacrament.

Earth's creatures
reaching out to hold
divinity.
Human vessels with
broken bread;
wine spilled out
Christ among his people.[6]

Because of the unique person that I am, my personality, character, gifts and strengths, I am a unique image or vessel containing and reflecting the grace of God. Even with my limits, I can celebrate God's goodness in me. Give thanks.

Bread and Wine

How does this bread "hold" or express for me the meaning of a life given so that others may be nourished? In what other ways may we taste the goodness of God? How is my family table an extension of the altar and this life-giving food?

When the Lord Jesus, shortly before he was betrayed,
took bread and wine as symbols of himself
and gave them to his disciples
he expressed himself perfectly:
bread that we might have life,
wine that we might be glad;
one bread, broken and shared in friendship,
one cup, pledge of a common destiny.
This bread is my body, which is for you;
this cup is my blood, poured out for you.

He is for us.
It is the story of his life.[7]

Jesus is "for us"; Jesus is for *me*. He desires for me the fullness of life, a heart filled with gladness. I pray and give thanks that I am so cherished, that in ordinary bread and wine, I am united with him and with his mystical body.

CHAPTER EIGHT

Times of the Day

In this chapter you will find a variety of prayers meant to be prayed during the various hours of the day. Some are contemporary expressions; others are timeless treasures from the tradition. You may find one that especially speaks to your own heart and choose to use that one regularly. You may prefer to choose a different prayer each day. Or, you may choose the following simple format that repeats itself for each day of the week: psalm, scripture text, intercessions, and blessing. Let the Spirit be your guide.

Prayers for the Morning

A Week of Morning Prayers

These prayers reflect a classic expression of daily prayer used by the Jewish people and later by Christians. Basic elements are the psalm, reading, the Canticle of Zachary, intercessions, and the Lord's Prayer. In this shorter version, we praise God (psalm), hear God's word (the reading), ask for what we need (intercessions), and pray the Lord's Prayer. You may wish to pray the gospel canticle (pages 148–149) following the reading.

SUNDAY

Take a few moments of quiet to be in touch with the Spirit of God within you and all about you. Ask for the grace to pray as who you are, at this moment, as you begin a new day. In your prayer, you become the voice of all creation, acknowledging the presence of God at all times, in all places.

Fill me with your love, O God.
May my whole being give you praise.

From Psalm 63

O God, you are my God, I seek you,
my soul thirsts for you;
my flesh faints for you,
as in a dry and weary land
where there is no water.
So I have looked upon you in the sanctuary,

beholding your power and glory.
Because your steadfast love is better than life,
my lips will praise you.
So I will bless you as long as I live;
I will lift up my hands and call on your name.
My soul is satisfied as with a rich feast,
and my mouth praises you with joyful lips
when I think of you on my bed,
and meditate on you in the watches of the night;
for you have been my help,
and in the shadow of your wings I sing for joy.
My soul clings to you;
your right hand upholds me.

Reading

> Do not fear, for I have redeemed you; I have called you by name, you are mine (Isaiah 43:1).

- Take a few moments to hear and to relish God's word to you today.
- Look ahead to what you know about the day before you.
- Ask God's grace that you may receive the day, its blessings and its challenges, with an open heart.
- Pray that God will be with you, especially when you need God's help.

Prayers of Intercession

For grateful hearts to sing the beauties of your creation and for the wisdom and the will to protect and conserve the riches of Earth, I pray:
Creator God, hear my prayer.

For willing and generous hands to share in setting the table where all can feast on Earth's bounty, I pray:
Creator God, hear my prayer.

For eyes to see the goodness in all persons—my family and friends, my neighbors, my coworkers, I pray:
Creator God, hear my prayer.

For a joyful spirit to spread hope and to bring merriment that all may know you are a God of love and of joy, I pray:
Creator God, hear my prayer.

(Here, you may name other persons and needs you carry in your heart. After naming these needs, pray slowly and attentively the Lord's Prayer.)

Blessing

Make the Sign of the Cross as you pray the blessing.

✠ May all creation give praise to our God every moment of this day! Amen.

MONDAY

Take a few moments of quiet, to be in touch with the Spirit of God within you and all about you. Ask for the grace to pray as who you are, at this moment, as you begin a new day. In your prayer, you become the voice of all creation acknowledging the presence of God at all times, in all places.

May all the earth give you glory, O God!
And break into song to offer praise!

Psalm 25

To you, O Lord, I lift up my soul.
O my God, in you I trust. . . .

Make me to know your ways, O Lord;
teach me your paths.
Lead me in your truth, and teach me,
for you are the God of my salvation;
for you I wait all day long.
Be mindful of your mercy,
O Lord, and of your steadfast love,
for they have been from of old.

Reading

I pray that you may have the power to comprehend, with all the saints, what is the breadth and length and height and depth, and to know the love of Christ that surpasses knowledge, so

> that you may be filled with all the fullness of God. (Ephesians 3:18–19)

- Take a few moments to hear and to relish God's word to you today.
- Look ahead to what you know about the day before you. Ask God's grace that you may receive the day, its blessings and its challenges, with an open heart.
- Pray that God will be with you, especially when you need God's help.

Prayers of Intercession

For fidelity to our baptismal call to live as the family of God, loving toward all,
Beloved God, hear our prayer.

For wise and effective governance in society and in the Church; for commitment to the common good,
Beloved God, hear our prayer.

For those who labor and offer their gifts for the well-being of all, especially for those in greatest need,
Beloved God, hear our prayer.

For those whose work is hidden and unnoticed, whose generous service builds up the Body of Christ,
Beloved God, hear our prayer.

(Here, you may name other persons and needs you carry in your heart. Then, pray slowly and attentively the Lord's Prayer.)

Blessing

Make the Sign of the Cross as you pray the blessing.

✠ May the light of Christ be with me, and shine through my words and works this day. Amen.

TUESDAY

Take a few moments of quiet, to be in touch with the Spirit of God within you and all about you. Ask for the grace to pray as who you are, at this moment, as you begin a new day. In your prayer, you become the voice of all creation acknowledging the presence of God at all times, in all places.

Companion God, you walk with us on life's journey.
Your word is a lamp for our feet and a light for our path.

Psalm 33:1–5, 21–22

Rejoice in the Lord, you righteous;
it is good for the just to sing praises.

Praise the Lord with the harp;
play upon the psaltery and lyre.
Sing for the Lord a new song;
sound a fanfare with all your skill upon the trumpet.

For your word, O Lord, is right,
and all your works are sure.
You love righteousness and justice;
your loving-kindness, O Lord, fills the whole earth.

Indeed, our heart rejoices in you,
for in your holy name we put our trust.

Let your loving-kindness, O Lord, be upon us,
as we have put our trust in you.[1]

Reading

> But Zion said, "The Lord has forsaken me, my Lord has forgotten me." Can a woman forget her nursing-child, or show no compassion for the child of her womb? Even these may forget, yet I will not forget you. See, I have inscribed you on the palms of my hands; your walls are continually before me." (Isaiah 49:14–16)

- Take a few moments to hear and to relish God's word to you today. Look ahead to what you know about the day before you. Ask God's grace that you may receive the day, its blessings and its challenges, with an open heart. Pray that God will be with you, especially when you need God's help.

Prayers of Intercession

For women and men of faith throughout the world,
that their lives may witness love and compassion,
Companion God, hear our prayer.

For the wisdom and the will to bring peace and build bridges, to reconcile and to renew the face of the earth,
Companion God, hear our prayer.

For the grace to live as one human family, by word and deed to reflect your great love for us,
Companion God, hear our prayer.

For a deeper awareness of your presence in our coming and going, at work and at rest, and in the surprising ways you meet us on the way,
Companion God, hear our prayer.

(Here, you may name other persons and needs you carry in your heart. Then, pray slowly and attentively the Lord's Prayer.)

Blessing

Make the Sign of the Cross as you pray the blessing.

✠ May God be with us and bless us in all that we do and say today. Amen.

WEDNESDAY

Take a few moments of quiet, to be in touch with the Spirit of God within you and all about you. Ask for the grace to pray as who you are, at this moment, as you begin a new day. In your prayer, you become the voice of all creation acknowledging the presence of God at all times, in all places.

Give thanks to our God, who is good,
whose great love surrounds us always.

Psalm 146:1–2, 5–8, 10

Praise the Lord!
Praise the Lord, O my soul!
I will praise the Lord as long as I live;
  I will sing praises to my God all my life long.

Happy are those whose help is the God of Jacob,
  whose hope is in the Lord their God,
who made heaven and earth,
  the sea, and all that is in them;
who keeps faith forever;
  who executes justice for the oppressed;
who gives food to the hungry.

The Lord sets the prisoners free;
the Lord opens the eyes of the blind.
The Lord lifts up those who are bowed down;
the Lord loves the righteous.

The Lord will reign forever,
your God, O Zion, for all generations.
Praise the Lord!

Reading

See what love the Father has given us, that we should be called children of God; and that is what we are. The reason the world does not know us is that it did not know him. (1 John 3:1)

Take a few moments to hear and to relish God's word to you today. Look ahead to what you know about the day before you. Ask God's grace that you may receive the day, its blessings and its challenges, with an open heart. Pray that God will be with you, especially when you need God's help.

Prayers of Intercession

For a world united in love, for an end to the curse of war and violence, we pray.
Gracious God, hear us.

For people of all religious beliefs and spiritual paths different from our own, for a deep respect among Christians, Muslims, and Jews, we pray.
Gracious God, hear us.

For racial harmony and full equality, and for a just sharing of Earth's bounty, we pray.
Gracious God, hear us.

For those in special need, the sick, the homebound and those who care for them, we pray.
Gracious God, hear us.

(Here, you may name other persons and needs you carry in your heart. Then, pray slowly and attentively the Lord's Prayer.)

Blessing

Make the Sign of the Cross as you pray the blessing.

✠ May God's blessing surround us this day, that we may bring that blessing to all whom we meet. Amen.

THURSDAY

Take a few moments of quiet, to be in touch with the Spirit of God within you and all about you. Ask for the grace to pray as who you are, at this moment, as you begin a new day. In your prayer, you become the voice of all creation acknowledging the presence of God at all times, in all places.

As the deer longs for running streams,
my soul longs for you, my God.

Canticle of Judith 16:13–15

I will sing to my God a new song:
O Lord, you are great and glorious,
wonderful in strength, invincible.
Let all your creatures serve you,
for you spoke, and they were made.
You sent forth your spirit, and it formed them;
there is none that can resist your voice.
For the mountains shall be shaken
to their foundations with the waters;
before your glance the rocks shall melt like wax.
But to those who fear you
you show mercy.

Reading

> But this is the covenant that I will make with the house of Israel after those days, says the Lord: I will put my law within them, and I will write it on their hearts; and I will be their God, and they shall be my people. (Jeremiah 31:33)

Take a few moments to hear and to relish God's word to you today. Look ahead to what you know about the day before you. Ask God's grace that you may receive the day, its blessings and its challenges, with an open heart. Pray that God will be with you, especially when you need God's help.

Prayers of Intercession

For leaders of nations, for those who govern in difficult times, for a recommitment to the common good of all peoples,
Provider-God, hear our prayer.

For justice and peace in all lands, for fair economic policy, respect for workers and for human rights,
Provider-God, hear our prayer.

For farmers and all who work the land, for fair weather and abundant crops that the hungry may be fed,
Provider-God, hear our prayer.

For infants, children, and the young, for nurturing families and communities to care for them that they may grow in wisdom, age, and grace,
Provider-God, hear our prayer.

(Here, you may name other persons and needs you carry in your heart. Then, pray slowly and attentively the Lord's Prayer.)

Blessing

Make the Sign of the Cross as you pray the blessing.

✠ May the peace of the living Christ fill our hearts, and may we share that peace with all whom we meet today. Amen.

FRIDAY

Take a few moments of quiet, to be in touch with the Spirit of God within you and all about you. Ask for the grace to pray as who you are, at this moment, as you begin a new day. In your prayer, you become the voice of all creation acknowledging the presence of God at all times, in all places.

Creator, reshape my heart,
to love as you love me.

Psalm 86

Incline your ear, O Lord, and answer me,
for I am poor and needy.

Preserve my life, for I am devoted to you;
    save your servant who trusts in you.
You are my God; be gracious to me, O Lord,
    for to you do I cry all day long.
Gladden the soul of your servant,
    for to you, O Lord, I lift up my soul.
For you, O Lord, are good and forgiving,
    abounding in steadfast love to all who call on you.
Give ear, O Lord, to my prayer;
    listen to my cry of supplication.
In the day of my trouble I call on you,
    for you will answer me.

Reading

> Everyone who thirsts, come to the waters; and you that have no money, come, buy and eat! Come, buy wine and milk without money and without price. Why do you spend your money for that which is not bread, and your labor for that which does not satisfy? Listen carefully to me, and eat what is good, and delight yourselves in rich food. (Isaiah 55:1–2)

Take a few moments to hear and to relish God's word to you today. Look ahead to what you know about the day before you. Ask God's grace that you may receive the day, its blessings and its challenges, with an open heart. Pray that God will be with you, especially when you need God's help.

Prayers of Intercession

As you, Jesus, suffer in the bodies of the sick, the elderly, the wounded,
help us to reach out to them with compassion and healing.

As you suffer in the bodies of those who are hungry, homeless, abandoned,
help us to find ways to provide food, shelter, and care.

As you suffer in the bodies of those wounded by war, those who are refugees and prisoners of conscience,
help us to reform unjust systems and free our sisters and brothers from all that destroys the human spirit.

As you suffer in the depths of those bound by mental illness, depression, fears,
help us to offer the refuge of understanding hearts, compassion, and welcome.

(Here, you may name other persons, needs you carry in your heart. Then, pray slowly and attentively the Lord's Prayer.)

Blessing

Make the Sign of the Cross as you pray the blessing.

✠ May God's blessing surround us this day, bringing deep peace and abundant joy.
Amen.

SATURDAY

Take a few moments of quiet to be in touch with the Spirit of God within you and all about you. Ask for the grace to pray as who you are, at this moment, as you begin a new day. In your prayer, you become the voice of all creation acknowledging the presence of God at all times, in all places.

Fill us at daybreak with your kindness;
today, let our hearts be glad!

Psalm 92

It is good to give thanks to the Lord,
to sing praises to your name, O Most High;
to declare your steadfast love in the morning,
and your faithfulness by night,
to the music of the lute and the harp,
to the melody of the lyre.
For you, O Lord, have made me glad by your work;
at the works of your hands I sing for joy.
How great are your works, O Lord!
Your thoughts are very deep!

Reading

For as the rain and the snow come down from heaven, and do not return there until they have watered the earth, making it bring forth and sprout, giving seed to the sower and bread to the eater, so shall my word be that goes out from

> my mouth; it shall not return to me empty, but it shall accomplish that which I purpose, and succeed in the thing for which I sent it. (Isaiah 55:10–11)

Take a few moments to hear and to relish God's word to you today. Look ahead to what you know about the day before you. Ask God's grace that you may receive the day, its blessings and its challenges, with an open heart. Pray that God will be with you, especially when you need God's help.

Prayers of Intercession

Loving God, I pray today in the spirit of Mary, valiant woman, faithful, and strong!
For discerning hearts to know your will for us, especially in difficult times,
Faithful God, hear our prayer.

For generosity as we attend to the daily demands that life asks of us and to the unplanned requests that others make of us,
Faithful God, hear our prayer.

For patience and peace, for willingness to trust even the questions in our lives, confident that your Spirit is with us,
Faithful God, hear our prayer.

For courage to face suffering, as did Mary at the foot of the cross, and to trust you will never leave us alone,
Faithful God, hear our prayer.

(Here, you may name other persons and needs you carry in your heart. Then, pray slowly and attentively the Lord's Prayer.)

Blessing

Make the Sign of the Cross as you pray the blessing.

✠ May the God of Jesus, Mary and Joseph bless us this day with peace and joy!
Amen.

A Selection of Short Morning Prayers

Variety and informality mark the morning prayers in this section. Many exhibit a refreshing simplicity from cultures and religious expressions other than our own.

Psalm 46:1–3, 10–11

In this prayer, the psalmist's unshakeable trust in God is dramatized with the use of cosmic disaster imagery.

God is our refuge and strength,
a very present help in trouble.
Therefore we will not fear,
though the earth should change,
though the mountains shake in the heart of the sea;
though its waters roar and foam,
though the mountains tremble with its tumult.

"Be still, and know that I am God!
I am exalted among the nations,
I am exalted in the earth."
The Lord of hosts is with us;
the God of Jacob is our refuge.

Psalm 100

I am joyful because the Lord is faithful and is with me all the days of my life, from my first breath until my last.

Be joyful in the Lord, all you lands;
serve the Lord with gladness
and come before God's presence with a song.

Know this: The Lord alone is God;
we belong to the Lord, who made us;
we are God's people and the sheep of God's pasture.
Enter God's gates with thanksgiving;
go into the holy courts with praise;
give thanks and call upon the name of the Lord.

For good is the Lord,
whose mercy is everlasting;
and whose faithfulness endures from age to age.[2]

Joy for a New Day

With a light and joyful heart, I welcome the new day.

> Waking up this morning, I smile.
> Twenty four brand new hours are before me.
> I vow to live fully in each moment
> and to look at all beings with eyes of compassion.[3]

Night's Passage to Day

I praise God for sleep and for waking, and ask for the privilege of sharing in God's work today.

> From the beauty of darkness
> to the beauty of light
> we come again, creating God,
> and from the praise of sleep
> to the praise of waking.
> Give us this day some portion in your work,
> for we are your image
> and so we must create
> what will be good in your sight.
> We ask this in Jesus' name,
> who is Lord for ever and ever. Amen.[4]

A Prayer of Thanks and Praise

I offer thanks and praise to the God of all creation, to Jesus, and to the Holy Spirit.

O God, you are the source of all creation.
Accept our morning thanks and praise.

We give you thanks for darkness and light,
which mark the rhythms of our lives,
for the sky that envelops and embraces us,
for the clouds that dance across the heavens,
for the oceans and the land,
for crafting us with ingenuity, beauty, and humor.
Accept our morning thanks and praise.

We give you thanks for Jesus,
sun of justice, bread of life, living water,
wisdom who played before you
in the beginning.
Accept our morning thanks and praise.

We give you thanks for the Holy Spirit,
promised gift who inspires us
with care for all creation.
Accept our morning thanks and praise.[5]

Morning Prayer for God's Help

In this prayer, I acknowledge my weakness and trust in God, whatever the day may bring.

O God, early in the morning I cry to you.
Help me to pray
And to concentrate my thoughts on you:
I cannot do this alone.

In me there is darkness,
But with you there is light;
I am lonely, but you do not leave me;
I am feeble in heart, but with you there is help.
I am restless, but with you there is peace.
In me there is bitterness, but with you there is patience;
I do not understand your ways,
But you know the way for me.
Restore me to liberty,
And enable me so to live now
that I may answer before you and before me.
Lord, whatever this day may bring,
Your name be praised.[6]

A Prayer to Do God's Work

In the words of this prayer, I ask that I become like Christ. Using the imagery of my baptismal garment, I pray that I may be clothed to serve my neighbor, following the example of Jesus.

God the Father, I give you thanks for all the marvels you have created.
I praise you and I bless you for the inestimable grace of life
that you give to us.
Transform me, make me a better Christian,
a living testimony of your mercy and of your power.

Strip me, Lord, of all roots of bitterness,
of false pride and haughtiness of heart.

Make me meek and humble of heart as was our Lord
Jesus Christ,
and never let me wound with my words or actions
the dignity of any person.
Put in my heart the ardent desire
to work earnestly for the poor and the needy.
Show me the garment with which you clothed me
the day that I received you as Lord and Savior of my
life.
May I wear those garments at the service of my
neighbor
and of this community.

Use me, Lord, for your work.[7]

A Prayer to Walk with God This Day

I pray to walk with my God this day, to pass the day in peace.

O God, you have let me pass the night in peace,
let me pass the day in peace.

Wherever I may go upon my way
which you made peaceable for me,
O God, lead my steps.
When I have spoken, keep lies away from me.
When I am hungry, keep me from murmuring.
When I am satisfied, keep me from pride.

Calling upon you, I pass the day,
O Lord, who has no lord.[8]

St. Patrick's Morning Prayer

In all things I pray that God act through me.

I sing as I arise today!
I call on my Creator's might:
the will of God to be my guide,
The eye of God to be my sight,
The word of God to be my speech,
The hand of God to be my stay,
The shield of God to be my strength,
The path of God to be my way.[9]

A Litany of Christ's Names

Begin your day with this simple litany, reflecting on the place of Christ in our faith tradition. The scriptures offer a variety of rich images of the Beloved One who in his words and works shows us the face of God.

Christ, firstborn of creation,
We tell of your glory (repeat after each invocation)
Christ, image of God,
Christ, gift of God,
Christ, love song of God,
Christ, morning star,
Christ, creating word,
Christ, liberating from bondage,
Christ, lighting our way,
Christ, caring for all in need,
Christ, reconciling all with God,
Christ, giving all your peace,

Christ, sending the creating Spirit,
Christ, loving justice,
Christ, the way, the truth and the life,
Christ, all in all.[10]

A Prayer for a Magnanimous Heart

In this simple and down-to-earth prayer, I ask to be my best self, and to "not forget to be kind."

Keep us, O God, from all pettiness,
Let us be large in thought, in word, in deed.
Let us be done with faultfinding
and leave off all self-seeking.
May we put away all pretense and meet each other face to face,
without self-pity and without prejudice.
May we never be hasty in judgment,
and always generous.
Let us always take time for all things,
and make us grow calm, serene and gentle.
Teach us to put into action our better impulses,
to be straightforward and unafraid.
Grant that we may realize
that it is the little things of life that create differences,
that in the big things of life we are as one.
And, O Lord God, let us not forget to be kind![11]

Prayers for Midday

As you pause at midday for food to satisfy your hunger, let your spirit breathe and also be nourished. If time and circumstances allow, you may wish to pray one of these prayers.

A Prayer to the Trinity at Midday

Take time, take time, to be mindful of God's Spirit that calms, heals, lives in you.

> Oh God, we take time to pause from daily work to gather our thoughts,
> to let our souls catch up with our bodies;
> to feel your presence in your creation;
> to ask forgiveness for our lapses, ours and on behalf of your people;
> and to be ourselves restored.
> *Breathing in, God's Spirit calms my body;*
> *breathing out, it's good to be alive.*
>
> Lord Jesus Christ, we take time to gather around you.
> By your life and teachings may we find our strength,
> and journeying together may we find our rest.
> *Breathing in, Christ lives in our lives;*
> *breathing out, it's good to be alive.*
>
> Holy Spirit, creative energy of love and compassion,
> life embracing, life transforming,
> heal our bodies, heal our souls, heal our relationships,

heal our nations.
Breathing in, the Spirit heals;
breathing out, it's good to be alive. Amen.[12]

Awareness of the Present Moment

The saint of "the little way," Thérèse of Lisieux, reminds me of the priceless present moment to love God: "I have only today."

My life is an instant
An hour which passes by;
My life is a moment
Which I have no power to stay
You know, O, my God,
That to love you here on earth—
I have only today.[13]

Prayer Despite Our Busy-ness

I pray to be mindful of God's presence, even in the midst of a hectic, busy life.

How is it, my God,
that you have given me
this hectic, busy life
that gives me so little time
to enjoy your presence.
I know that you are
constantly beside me,

yet I am usually so busy
that I ignore you.
If you want me to
remain so busy,
please help me
to think about and love you
even in the midst of
such hectic activity. Amen.[14]

A Light-Hearted Prayer

Despite the hurried life I live, I pray for sanity, good sense, and wisdom.

Creator of the world, keep me sane,
Keep my sense and wisdom, until
You come for me.[15]

Lunch Blessing

In the kitchen I remember all that I have been given which nourishes me, so much given through my mother. Grateful for these gifts, I share them with others.

Bless my [day] with moments of joy.
Bless the calloused hands of migrant workers.
Bless the flour-covered fingers of bakers.
Bless the texture and pleasing aromas of food.
Bless those who gather.
Bless the breaking of bread.

Blessed Be! Blessed Be! Blessed Be!
Christ at every table, Christ beside me,
Christ behind me,
Christ around me,
In the breaking of the bread.[16]

Prayers for the Evening

From this collection of prayers at the close of day, you may choose a different one each night, or you may find a favorite that you'll pray again and again. Pray as the Spirit within draws you.

Prayer at Nightfall

The following prayer reflects the texts of Compline, the traditional night prayer of Christians. Prayed by women and men of faith for centuries, night prayer at its heart expresses trust in God's provident care of us.

Protect us, O God, while we are awake; watch over us as we sleep,
that awake, we may keep watch with Christ, and asleep, rest in his peace.

Pause for a few moments now to review your day—God's presence with you in blessing and your response to God's gifts. Where you are aware of failing, ask pardon. Recall God's gifts, and give thanks.

Psalm 134

Come, bless the Lord, all you servants of the Lord,
who stand by night in the house of the Lord!
Lift up your hands to the holy place,
and bless the Lord.

May the Lord, maker of heaven and earth,
bless you from Zion.

Reading

But you, beloved, are not in darkness, for that day to surprise you like a thief; for you are all children of light and children of the day; we are not of the night or of darkness. So then let us not fall asleep as others do, but let us keep awake. . . . (1Thessalonians 5:4–6)

Simeon's Canticle: Luke 2:29–32 (Nunc Dimittis)

From the Liturgy of the Hours.

Now, Lord, you let your servant go in peace;
your word has been fulfilled:
my own eyes have seen the salvation,
which you have prepared in the sight of every people:
a light to reveal you to the nations
and the glory of your people Israel.
Glory to the Father, to the Son and to the Holy Spirit;

as it was in the beginning is now and will be forever.
Amen.

Prayer

Surround this house, loving God, with your compassion and care.
May restful sleep bring refreshment,
that we may awaken to a new day
eager to serve you, in all the ways that you come to us.
In Jesus' name, we pray. Amen.

Blessing

Make the Sign of the Cross as you pray the blessing.

✠ May God give us restful sleep and at the end, a peaceful death.
Amen.

Psalm 86:1–7, 11–12

Hear your servant, my God; gladden my heart and teach me your ways.

Incline your ear, O Lord, and answer me,
for I am poor and needy.
Preserve my life, for I am devoted to you;
save your servant who trusts in you.
You are my God; be gracious to me, O Lord,
for to you do I cry all day long.

Gladden the soul of your servant,
for to you, O Lord, I lift up my soul.
For you, O Lord, are good and forgiving,
abounding in steadfast love
to all who call on you.
Give ear, O Lord, to my prayer;
listen to my cry of supplication.
In the day of my trouble I call on you
for you will answer me.

Teach me your way, O Lord,
that I may walk in our truth;
give me an undivided heart to
revere your name.
I give thanks to you, O Lord my God,
with my whole heart
and I will glorify your name forever.

Psalm 91:1–2, 5–6, 14–16

This psalm expresses deep trust in God, who promises to answer us and show us the fullness of life. Select one or more of these verses to read prayerfully. Which ones speak to your heart?

You who live in the shelter of the Most High,
who abide in the shadow of the Almighty,
will say to the Lord, "My refuge and my fortress;
my God, in whom I trust."

You will not fear the terror of the night,
or the arrow that flies by day,
or the pestilence that stalks in darkness
or the destruction that wastes at noonday.

Those who love me, I will deliver;
I will protect those who know my name.
When they call to me, I will answer them;
I will be with them in trouble.
I will rescue them and honor them.
With long life I will satisfy them,
and show them my salvation.

Trust in God

In the simplicity of this prayer, I ask for peace at night, as I have spent the day in peace.

O God, you have let me pass this day in peace,
let me pass the night in peace.
O Lord, who has no lord,
there is no strength but in you.

You alone have no obligation.
Under your hand I pass the night.
You are my mother and my father.[17]

Prayer for Protection, Pardon, Blessing

Drawing together the needs of body and spirit, for self and others, in trust I lay all these concerns at the feet of my God.

Protect me and my loved ones tonight, O blessed One.
Keep us away from harm and danger.
Let our sleep be peaceful so that we awake in the morning
refreshed in body and mind.

If I have strayed from the true path, may I never do so again.
If I have carelessly hurt someone today, by word or deed,
may I be more mindful the next time.
May my actions reflect your love and compassion.
I shall strive to cleanse my heart from hate and envy,
and live in harmony with all people.
Whatever wrong someone may do to me,
may I be compassionate and forgive
and bear no hatred in my heart.
I shall be grateful for the acts of love and consideration shown to me,
no matter how small they appear to be.
For those I love, and for those who love me,
may this life be a blessing and a source of happiness to all beings.

May we be blessed with good health, strength, peace
and happiness.
May my parents, brothers and sisters, teachers,
friends and relatives
be well and happy.
May all living beings including my enemies find
peace.[18]

A Hebrew Prayer at Evening

I praise God for daylight and dusk, for time and seasons. The evening twilight invites reflection on life's mysteries.

Bless Adonai
who spins day into dusk
With wisdom watch
the dawn gates open;
with understanding let
time and seasons
come and go;
with awe perceive the stars in lawful orbit.

Morning dawns,
evening darkens;
darkness and light yielding
one to the other,
yet each distinguished
and unique.

Marvel at Life!
Strive to know its ways!
Seek Wisdom and Truth,
the gateways
to life's mysteries!

Wondrous indeed
is the evening twilight.[19]

Coming Home at Day's End

To know that we come home to God at the ending of each day—what a blessing! What a joy!

At the day's end we come home to you, O God,
with much or little to show for this day
lived in the light of your gospel.
Give us shelter and refresh us with your love
that we might give as freely as we have received.
We pray in Jesus' name,
who is Lord for ever and ever. Amen.[20]

Prayer for God's Presence All Our Days

Each day is an image of the totality of life. I pray to be with God at journey's end.

May God support us all the day long
till the shades lengthen

and the evening comes
and the busy world is hushed
and the fever of life is over
and our work is done.
Then in mercy may God give us a safe lodging
and a holy rest and peace at the last.[21]

Prayer for Angels to Be Near

The image of angels guarding the sleeping world expresses trust in the caring presence of God.

Dear God,
I give to you this night.
Post angels round my home,
my bed,
my children,
my loves,
and everyone.
Send angels through the world tonight,
to heal the sick
and awaken the dead.
Let miracles replace the pain
in all of us.
Lay Your hands on all our eyes,
that we might see
at last. Amen.[22]

Celtic Prayer at Day's End

I pray that God may bless the story of my day and send the Spirit to guard and protect me.

Through dark nights and ages,
Our ancestors lit their night fires.
They gathered around the circle
Telling their tales of the day.
O God, source of all holy fires,
Bless the story of my day.
Enlighten and warm my heart.
O God, send out your Spirit—
A tongue of fire above my head.
Let not the wick be quashed,
Nor the bruised reed trampled.[23]

St. Patrick's Hymn at Evening

May angels be near; may we sleep in peace; may the work of the day be blessed.

O Christ, Son of the living God,
May your holy angels guard our sleep.
May they watch us as we rest
And hover around our beds.
Let them reveal to us in our dreams
Visions of your glorious truth,
O High Prince of the universe,
O High Priest of the mysteries.

May no dreams disturb our rest
And no nightmares darken our dreams.
May no fears or worries delay
Our willing, prompt repose.
May the virtue of our daily work
Hallow our nightly prayers.
May our sleep be deep and soft,
Our work be fresh and hard.[24]

Night Prayer

How Precious to Me

I fall asleep at night remembering God's love and God's gifts.

How precious to me is your steadfast love, O God!
I take refuge in the shadow of your wings
and feast on the abundance of your table.
I depend on the river of your gifts.
For with you is the fountain of life;
only in your light do I see light. Amen.[25]

Prayer that God Keep Watch

Be with us, O God. Be with all in need. You love us all.

Keep watch, dear Lord,
with those who work, or watch, or weep this night,
and give thine angels charge over those who sleep.
Tend the sick, Lord Christ;

give rest to the weary,
bless the dying,
soothe the suffering,
pity the afflicted,
shield the joyous;
and all for thy love's sake.[26]

PART FOUR

An Invitation to Feasts and Seasons

These special seasons of the Christian year draw from the rich texts of scripture. Each of the following sections offers scripture texts, prayers, and brief reflections in the spirit of the season.

CHAPTER NINE

Advent

The Scriptures of Advent

Isaiah 11:1–4

A shoot shall come out from the stump of Jesse,
And a branch shall grow out of his roots.
The Spirit of the Lord shall rest on him,
the spirit of wisdom and understanding,
the spirit of counsel and might,
the spirit of knowledge and the fear of the Lord.
His delight shall be in the fear of the Lord.

He shall not judge by what his eyes see,
    or decide by what his ears hear;
but with righteousness he shall judge the poor,
    and decide with equity for the meek of the earth.

Isaiah 40:1–5

Comfort, O comfort my people,
    says your God.
Speak tenderly to Jerusalem, and cry to her
that she has served her term, that her penalty is paid,
that she has received from the Lord's hand
double for all her sins.

A voice cries out:
"In the wilderness prepare the way of the Lord,
make straight in the desert a highway for our God.
Every valley shall be lifted up,
and every mountain and hill be made low;
the uneven ground shall become level,
and the rough places a plain.
Then the glory of the Lord shall be revealed,
and all people shall see it together,
for the mouth of the Lord has spoken."

Isaiah 61:1–2, 11

The Spirit of the Lord God is upon me,
because the Lord has anointed me;
he has sent me to bring good news to the oppressed,

to bind up the broken-hearted,
to proclaim liberty to the captives,
and release to the prisoners;
to proclaim the year of the Lord's favor,
and the day of vengeance of our God;
to comfort all who mourn.

For as the earth brings forth its shoots,
and as a garden causes what is sown in it to spring up,
so the Lord God will cause righteousness and praise
to spring up before all the nations.

Romans 13:11–12

Besides this, you know what time it is, how it is now the moment for you to wake from sleep. For salvation is nearer to us now than when we became believers; the night is far gone, the day is near. Let us then lay aside the works of darkness and put on the armor of light. . . .

Psalm 80:1–3

Give ear, O Shepherd of Israel, you who lead Joseph like a flock!
You who are enthroned upon the cherubim,
shine forth . . .
Stir up your might, and come to save us!

Restore us, O God; let your face shine, that we may be saved.

Mark 1:1–3

The beginning of the good news of Jesus Christ, the Son of God. As it is written in the prophet Isaiah,
"See, I am sending my messenger ahead of you,
who will prepare your way;
the voice of one crying out in the wilderness:
'Prepare the way of the Lord,
make his paths straight.'"

Luke 1:30–35, 38

The angel said to [Mary], "Do not be afraid, Mary, for you have found favor with God. And now, you will conceive in your womb and bear a son, and you will name him Jesus. He will be great, and will be called the Son of the Most High, and the Lord God will give to him the throne of his ancestor David. He will reign over the house of Jacob forever, and of his kingdom there will be no end." Mary said to the angel, "How can this be, since I am a virgin?" The angel said to her, "The Holy Spirit will come upon you, and the power of the Most High will overshadow you; therefore the child to be born will be holy; he will be called Son of God. . . . Then Mary said, "Here am I, the servant of the Lord; let it be with me according to your word."

The Prayers of Advent

Advent Daily Prayer

The following can be used as a daily Advent morning prayer; you may choose a different reading each day, perhaps one of the readings for the Eucharist of the day.

To you, O God, I lift up my soul;
O my God, in you I trust.

Psalm 86

Incline your ear, O Lord, and answer me.
for I am poor and needy.
Preserve my life, for I am devoted to you;
save your servant who trusts in you.
You are my God; be gracious to me, O Lord,
for to you do I cry all day long.
Gladden the soul of your servant,
for to you, O Lord, I lift my soul.
For you, O Lord, are good and forgiving,
abounding in steadfast love to all who call on you.
Give ear, O Lord, to my prayer;
listen to my cry of supplication.
In the day of my trouble I call on you,
for you will answer me.

Reading

Be patient, therefore, beloved, until the coming of the Lord. The farmer waits for the precious crop from the earth, being patient with it until it receives the early and the late rains. You also must be patient. Strengthen your hearts, for the coming of the Lord is near. (James 5:7–8)

You may choose a different reading, for example, from the Mass of the day.

Prayers

God, in whom we live and move and have our being,
come and show us how to love as you love.
Father-Mother of the poor, consoler of the afflicted,
set captives free and comfort those who sorrow.
Desire of every human heart, in this season of giving,
help us to know again that you alone satisfy our longings.
You are not far away; we need not seek you in the heavens;
you live in the depths of our being, in our sisters and brothers, in all of creation.[1]

(Here you may name other persons and needs you carry in your heart. Then, pray slowly and attentively the Lord's Prayer.)

Blessing

Make the Sign of the Cross as you pray the blessing.

✠ May God, the all Holy One, bless this day with peace, that we may bear that peace to all whom we meet. Amen.[2]

An Ancient Advent Hymn

Creator of the stars of night,
your people's everlasting light,
O Christ, Redeemer of us all,
we pray you hear us when we call.[3]

Late Have I Loved You

Late have I loved you, O Beauty so ancient and so new; late have I loved you. For behold you were within me, and I outside; and I sought you outside and in my unloveliness fell upon those lovely things that you have made. You were with me, and I was not with you. I was kept from you by those things, yet had they not been in you, they would not have been at all. You called and cried to me to break open my deafness and you sent forth your beams and you shone upon me and chased away my blindness. You breathed fragrance upon me, and I drew in my breath and do now pant for you. I tasted you, and now hunger and thirst for you. You touched me, and I have burned for your peace.[4]

The "O Antiphons"

In the last days before Christmas (December 17–24), we join with Christians around the world and pray the great "O Antiphons." We address Christ in titles emerging from the richness of the Hebrew tradition. The antiphons express our great longing for the coming of the Messiah. The texts are from a ninth-century Latin hymn; we recognize the familiar Advent hymn, "O Come, O Come Emmanuel."

O come, O Wisdom from on high,
Who orders all things mightily;
To us the path of knowledge show,
And teach us in her ways to go.

O come, O come, great Lord of might,
Who to your tribes on Sinai's height
In ancient times once gave the Law
In cloud and majesty and awe.

O come, O Rod of Jesse's stem,
From every foe deliver them
That trust your mighty power to save,
And give them victory o'er the grave.

O come, O Key of David, come,
And open wide our heavenly home;
Make safe the way that leads on high,
And close the path to misery.

O come, O Dayspring from on high
And cheer us by your drawing nigh;
Disperse the gloomy clouds of night,
And death's dark shadow put to flight.

O come, Desire of nations, bind
In one the hearts of [human] kind;
O bid our sad divisions cease,
And be for us our king of peace.

O come, O come, Emmanuel,
And ransom captive Israel,
That mourns in lonely exile here
Until the Son of God appear.[5]

To Mary

Mother of Christ,
our hope and patroness,
star of the sea, our beacon in distress.
Guide to the shores of everlasting day
God's holy people on their pilgrim way.

Virgin, in you God made his dwelling place;
Mother of all the living, full of grace,
blessed are you: God's word you did believe;
"Yes" on your lips undid the "No" of Eve.

Daughter of God, who bore his holy One,
dearest of all to Christ, your loving Son,

show us his face, O Mother, as on earth,
loving us all, you gave our Savior birth.[6]

Gather Us

Lord Jesus Christ,
by love's decree you became human
like one of us
in order to establish a community of faith
and fellowship.
Gather all nations and people into your church
and make it a city of justice and peace
for the good of the whole human family.
We ask this in your holy name.
Amen.[7]

Spring Forth from Within Us

We do not pray that your birth according to the flesh shall be renewed as it once occurred upon this day. Rather do we pray that your invisible Godhead may be grafted into us. May that which was then accorded after the flesh to Mary alone now be granted in the spirit to the church; that faith unquestioning may conceive you, the spirit free of all corruption may bear you, the soul over-shadowed by the power of the Most High may quicken with you evermore. Go not forth from us; spring forth rather from within us.[8]

Words That Invite Reflection

Use these passages as an entry into deeper reflection and prayer on the spirit of the Advent season.

The Visitation of God

> The "Visitation" of God is the experience of God's presence, the Ultimate Mystery making Itself known in the Word made flesh. This is the meaning of the Christmas-Epiphany celebration. . . . The Christmas-Epiphany Mystery is the celebration of the transmission of divine light. The liturgical season begins with Advent, a period of intense preparation.[9]

The Life Within

> When a woman is carrying a child she develops a certain instinct of self-defense. It is not selfishness; it is not egoism. It is an absorption into the life within, a folding of self like a little tent around the child's frailty, a God-like instinct to cherish, and some day to bring forth the life. A closing upon it like the petals of a flower closing upon the dew that shines in its heart. This is precisely the attitude we must have to Christ, the life within us, in the Advent of our contemplation. . . . By his own will Christ was dependent on Mary during Advent: He was absolutely helpless; He could go nowhere but where she chose to take Him; He could not speak; her breathing was his breath; His heart beat in the beating of her heart.[10]

To Watch for Christ

They watch for Christ
who are sensitive, eager, apprehensive in mind,
who are awake, alive, quick-sighted,
zealous in honoring him,
who look for him in all that happens, and
who would not be surprised,
who would not be over-agitated or overwhelmed,
if they found that he was coming at once. . . .

This then is to watch:
to be detached from what is present, and
to live in what is unseen;
to live in the thought of Christ as he came once,
and as he will come again;
to desire his second coming, from our affectionate
and grateful remembrance of his first.[11]

Seeing as God Sees

By virtue of the Creation and, still more, of the Incarnation, *nothing* here below is *profane* for those who know how to see.[12]

CHAPTER TEN

Christmas

The Scriptures of Christmas

Psalm 96:1–3, 11–13

O sing to the Lord a new song;
sing to the Lord, all the earth.
Sing to the Lord, bless his name;
tell of his salvation from day to day.
Declare his glory among the nations,
his marvelous works among all the peoples.

Let the heavens be glad, and let the earth rejoice;
let the sea roar, and all that fills it;
let the field exult, and everything in it.
Then shall all the trees of the forest sing for joy
before the Lord; for he is coming,
for he is coming to judge the earth.

[The Lord] will judge the world with righteousness
and the peoples with his truth.

Micah 5:2, 4–5

But you, O Bethlehem of Ephrathah, who are one of the little clans of Judah,
from you shall come forth for me one who is to rule in Israel,
whose origin is from of old, from ancient days.

And he shall stand and feed his flock in the strength of the Lord,
in the majesty of the name of the Lord his God.
And they shall live secure,
for now he shall be great to the ends of the earth;
and he shall be the one of peace.

Wisdom 18:14–15

For while gentle silence enveloped all things,
and night in its swift course was now half gone,
your all-powerful word leapt from heaven,
from the royal throne. . . .

Luke 2:8–14

In that region there were shepherds living in the fields, keeping watch over their flock by night. Then an angel of the Lord stood before them, and the glory of the Lord shone around them, and they were terrified. But the angel said to them, "Do not be afraid; for see—I am bringing you good news of great joy for all the people: to you is born this day in the city of David a Savior, who is the Messiah, the Lord. This will be a sign for you: you will find a child wrapped in bands of cloth and lying in a manger." And suddenly there was with the angel a multitude of the heavenly host, praising God and saying,
"Glory to God in the highest heaven,
and on earth peace among those whom he favors."

John 1:14, 16–18

And the Word became flesh and lived among us, and we have seen his glory, the glory as of a father's only son, full of grace and truth.

From his fullness we have all received, grace upon grace. The law indeed was given through Moses; grace and truth came through Jesus Christ. No one has ever seen God. It is God the only Son, who is close to the Feather's heart, who has made him known.

1 John 1:1-4

We declare to you what was from the beginning,
what we have heard,
what we have seen with our eyes,
what we have looked at and touched with our hands,
concerning the word of life—
this life was revealed,
and we have seen it and testify to it,
and declare to you the eternal life
that was with the Father and was revealed to us—
we declare to you what we have seen and heard
so that you also may have fellowship with us;
and truly our fellowship is with the Father
and with his Son Jesus Christ.
We are writing these things so that our joy may be complete.

The Prayers of Christmas

Mary's Prayer

Join your prayer to that of Mary as you contemplate the infant Christ.

O my child, child of sweetness,
How is it that I hold thee, Almighty?
And how that I feed thee,
Who givest bread to all?
How is it that I swaddle thee,
Who with the clouds encompasseth the whole earth?[1]

Earth's Gift to God

In the following two prayers, I celebrate and honor Mary, mother of God. Through her, God's greatest gift comes to me.

What shall we present unto thee, O Christ,
For thy coming to earth for us?
Each of thy creatures brings thee a thank-offering:
the Angels—singing; the heavens—a star;
The wise men—treasures; the shepherds—devotion;
The earth—a cave; the desert—a manger;
But we offer thee the virgin-mother.[2]

Grace-filled, unspotted, God-bearing virgin,
holy your womb: Emmanuel lay in it.
You fed at your breast the food of the world.
What praise can reach you, what glory touch you?
Hail, God's mother, delight of the angels;
hail full of grace, foretold by prophets' preaching.
The Lord is with you. The child you bore has saved the world.[3]

A Prayer That Christ Be Born in Us

At this season when we celebrate Christ's birth, I pray that Christ be born in me, that I may love as he loves.

Be born in us,
Incarnate Love.
Take our flesh and blood,

and give us your humanity;
take our lives, and give us your vision;
take our minds,
and give us your pure thought;
take our feet and set them in your path;
take our hands
and fold them in your prayer;
take our hearts
and give them your will to love.[4]

We Didn't Know You

In this lovely carol, in the tradition of African American spirituals, I acknowledge that though Jesus came among us, "we didn't know who you was."

Sweet little Jesus Boy,
They made you be born in a manger.
Dear little holy child,
And they didn't know who you was.
Didn't know you came to save us, Lord,
To take our sins away.
Our eyes were blind, we could not see.
We didn't know who you was.

Long time ago, you was born,
Born in a manger low,
Sweet little Jesus Boy.
The world treat you mean, Lord.
Treat me too,
But that's how things is down here.
We didn't know 'twas you!

Sweet little Jesus Boy,
Born long time ago,
Dear little holy child,
And we didn't know who you was![5]

Praying with a Favorite Carol

In this season of such beautiful music, choose a favorite carol to be subject of your contemplation of the Christmas mystery. Prepare a space using a candle or candles, an image of the Nativity scene, even the Christmas tree, our tree of life. Quiet your heart—choose a time early in the morning when the day's activity has not yet begun, or later in the evening when the day has run its course.

Recall the unbelievable gift of God's great love revealed in Jesus, the Christ. Hear anew the Christmas carol which you have chosen . . . Be with this mystery . . . Give thanks . . . and let your spirit rest in hope—with God, all things are possible, all things are love.

Blessing of a Home (Epiphany Tradition)

An early Christian custom observed on the feast of the Epiphany is to mark the lintel in chalk with the numbers of the New Year (20 + 12) along with the initials of the Magi—C for Caspar, M for Melchior, and B for Balthasar.

The leader begins with the Sign of the Cross, and then says:

It is in the home that the first experience of love occurs; it is here that love is nurtured and grows to maturity. The Christian home is also the ground for much of our spiritual growth. We read in the gospels that the ministry of Jesus occurs in many different homes. To hallow our home as an environment for nurture and renewal is a way of beginning the New Year in a deeply Christian way. The blessing of our home encourages us to dedicate our lives at home to God and to others.

One person takes chalk and marks on the lintel of the front door:

20 + C + M + B + 12

While this goes on, another reads:

The Three Wise Men,
Caspar,
Melchior, and
Balthasar
followed the star of God's Son who became human
two thousand
and (twelve) years ago.

✠ May Christ bless our home
✠ and remain with us throughout the New Year. Amen.

Reader 2:

May all who come to our home this year rejoice to find Christ living among us, and may we seek and serve, in everyone we meet, that same Jesus who is the Incarnate Word, now and forever. May we be blessed with health, goodness of heart, gentleness; and may we abide in God's will. We ask this through Christ our Savior. Amen.

C M B above a door also stands for *Christus Mansionem Benedicat,* Latin for "May Christ Bless this house."

If you wish, you may then move through the house and sprinkle each room with holy water. You may also plan for sharing simple refreshments at the end.[6]

Words That Invite Reflection

Use these passages as an entry into deeper reflection on the spirit of the season of Christmas.

God Comes Gently, Always in Love

How small and gentle his coming was. He came as an infant. The night in which he came was noisy and crowded; it is unlikely that, in the traffic and travelers to Bethlehem, the tiny wail of the newly born could be heard.

God approaches gently, often secretly, always in love, never through violence and fear. He comes to us, as God has told us, in those whom we know in our own lives. Very often we do not recognize God. God comes in many people we do not like, in all who need what we can give, in all who have something to give us; and for our great comfort. God comes in those we love. In our fathers and mothers, our brothers and sisters, our friends and our children. Because this is so, we may not be content ever to love with only *natural* love. We must also love everyone with a *supernatural, sacramental* love. We must love Christ in them with Christ's love in us. It would be well if those seeking perfection ceased trying so painstakingly to learn how *not* to love and learned instead how to love well.[7]

Christmas, the Beginning of a Wondrous Mystery

The feast of Christmas is the first burst of light in the unfolding of the Christmas-Epiphany Mystery. Theologically, Christmas is the revelation of the Eternal Word made flesh. But it takes time to celebrate and penetrate all that this event actually contains and involves. The most we can do on Christmas night is gasp in wonderment and rejoice with the angels and the shepherds who first experienced it. The various aspects of the Mystery of divine light are examined one by one in the days following Christmas.[8]

Lo, How a Rose E'er Blooming

Lo, how a rose e'er blooming
From tender stem hath sprung
Of Jesse's lineage coming
as prophets long have sung.
It came a flow'ret bright
Amid the cold of winter
When half spent was the night.

Isaiah 'twas foretold it
The rose I have in mind.
With Mary we behold it
The Virgin mother kind.
To show God's love aright
She bore to us a savior
When half spent was the night.[9]

A Mother's Unique Gift

The comfort that a mother can give in early life is like no other comfort that a child ever experiences before or after. The attachment, the need, the sense of identification and security inherent in maternal contact makes the female figure a sign and symbol of mercy and comfort, of relief and joy . . .

Mother and child, the virgin and child, have appealed to more than just artists. Mary as mother and as Our Lady of Peace and Mercy has had a primal power on believers through the ages. We still long for our mother's care like infants crying in the night. Since the understanding of God as mother has been suppressed in Western Christian tradition, the experience of Mary as mother has been accentuated and fulfilled the ideal and symbol of maternal mercy and love. . . .

We are confirmed by Mary, who as a merciful mother and the handmaid of the Lord assures us that we will not be left with a deep anxiety within, or a fear of the total otherness and power beyond ourselves. Fear of the sacred and the natural awe of God has been complemented by a final mercy and reassurance.[10]

The Babe Grown Man . . . Our Savior

We can keep all our modern, beloved Christmas trappings, as long as we see through them and as long as we know that there is a reality and a future behind those things of the past. When we celebrate Midnight Mass in Bethlehem "at the crib," as the missal says; when we go as good pilgrims to the Mass "at dawn" in the Church of the *Anastasis* (Resurrection); and when we see the full glory of the divine child in the third Mass, we have already made a seven-league step from the crib idyll toward the full meaning of the parousia.

. . . Certainly our crib and customs have their place, and nobody will take them away; but their place is the foreground, the emotional, historical, meditative side of our religious being. Still while the world moves on in powerful strides and groans for redemption, let us not forget that it was not the babe who redeemed it, but the babe grown man, crucified, resurrected, and sitting at the right hand of the Father, whence he will come to *judge* the living and the dead.[11]

The Christmas-Epiphany Mystery: The Challenge to Live in the Light

In the light of the Christmas-Epiphany Mystery, we perceive that union with Christ is not some kind of spiritual happy hour. It is a war with the powers of evil that killed Jesus and that might kill us, too, if we get in their way. Because we live in the human condition, the divine light is constantly being challenged by the repressive and regressive forces within us as individuals and within society, neither of which wants to hear about love, certainly not about self-giving love. The Gospel message of service is not one that is easily heard. Hence, we need to deepen and nourish our faith through a liturgy that empowers us with the energy to go on showing love no matter what happens. This power is communicated to us in the Christmas-Epiphany Mystery according to our present receptive capacity.[12]

CHAPTER ELEVEN

Lent

The Scriptures of Lent

Deuteronomy 30:15, 19–20

See, I have set before you today life and prosperity, death and adversity.

. . . I call heaven and earth to witness against you today that I have set before you life and death, blessings and curses. Choose life so that you and your descendants may live, loving the lord your God, obeying him, and holding fast to him; for that means life to you and length of days. . . .

Isaiah 58:6–11

Is this not the fast that I choose:
to loose the bonds of injustice,
to undo the thongs of the yoke,
to let the oppressed go free,
and to break every yoke?
Is it not to share your bread with the hungry,
and bring the homeless poor into your house;
when you see the naked, to cover them,
and not to hide yourself from your own kin?
Then your light shall break forth like the dawn,
and your healing shall spring up quickly;
your vindicator shall go before you,
the glory of the Lord shall be your rear guard.
Then you shall call, and the Lord will answer;
you shall cry for help, and he will say, Here I am.

Mark 1:15

Repent, and believe in the good news.

Matthew 5:24

First be reconciled to your brother or sister, and then come and offer your gift.

Matthew 4:4

One does not live by bread alone, but
by every word that comes
from the mouth of God.

Matthew 10:38–39

Whoever does not take up the cross and follow me is not worthy of me. Those who find their life will lose it, and those who lose their life for my sake will find it.

1 Corinthians 13:1

If I speak in the tongues of mortals and angels, but do not have love, I am a noisy gong or a clanging cymbal.

The Prayers of Lent

Lenten Daily Prayer

You may choose to use this prayer often during Lent, while selecting a different reading, perhaps one of the readings from the liturgy of the day.

Seek the Lord, who longs to be found.
Call upon your God who is very near.

Psalm 51:1–2, 10–12, 15

Have mercy on me, O God,
according to your steadfast love;
according to your abundant mercy
blot out my transgressions.
Wash me thoroughly from my iniquity,
and cleanse me from my sin.

Create in me a clean heart, O God,
and put a new and right spirit within me.
Do not cast me away from your presence,
and do not take your holy spirit from me.
Restore to me the joy of your salvation,
and sustain in me a willing spirit.

O Lord, open my lips,
and my mouth will declare your praise.

Reading

Thus says the Lord of hosts . . . This command I gave them, "Obey my voice, and I will be your God, and you shall be my people; and walk only in the way that I command you, so that it may be well with you." (Jeremiah 7:21, 23)

(You may also choose a reading from the Mass of the day.)

Reflect for a few moments on these sacred words, and ask the Spirit to remind you of them often through the day. You may wish to pray the morning canticle (see pages 148–149).

Prayers of Intercession

One with Jesus, our light in the darkness, we offer our prayer.
Shelter your people with peace.
Renew in wisdom and courage all those entrusted with leadership in the Church and in the world;
may they guide your people with humility, integrity and vision.
Help us to walk the way of selfless giving
and faithfully follow Jesus our companion and guide.
Enfold with gentleness those burdened and afraid;
may they rest with hope for a new day.[1]

I pray also for these needs . . .
Reverently, slowly, pray the Lord's Prayer

Concluding Prayer

Merciful God, you hear the cries of the poor;
the lowly in spirit you save;
the broken of heart you embrace.
Have compassion on us in our need.
Answer us and bring us your peace.
Amen.[2]

Blessing

As you pray the blessing, make the Sign of the Cross.

✠ May the living God walk with us, all through the moments of this day. Amen.

Lent, the Acceptable Time

This prayer reminds me of what Lent means as I journey with Christ toward Easter.

Loving God, you tell us that this is the "acceptable time,"
this is the "day of salvation."
Help us in this holy season
to be faithful to our Baptismal promises:
that you be the center of our living,
that Christ be the pattern of our loving.
May our deeds of prayer, fasting and good works
renew us as a people of fidelity and love.
In Jesus' name, we pray. Amen.

Prayer for God's Blessing on Our Lenten Efforts

At the beginning of Lent, I remember the traditional Christian practices of the season—prayer, fasting, and almsgiving—and the meaning they continue to carry for the faith community today.

Lord Jesus, make us a new creation.
Lord, hear our prayer.

Lord Jesus, renew our hearts and our minds according to the pattern of the Gospel
Lord, hear our prayer.

Lord Jesus, remake the world and reconcile it to God:
Lord, hear our prayer.
Lord Jesus, renew and refresh your church in the power of the Holy Spirit:
Lord, hear our prayer.

Lord Jesus, grant life and peace to the faithful departed:
Lord, hear our prayer.

By the prayers of your holy Mother and of all your saints:
Lord, hear our prayer.

Abba, loving Father,
your Son fasted and prayed forty days,
preparing himself to do your will.
May our Lenten self-denial purge us from sin
and prepare us for a life of testimony and service,
through the same Christ our Lord.
Amen.[3]

Praying with the Cross

Take an image of the Crucified One—a picture, an icon, or a crucifix—and slowly, prayerfully ponder these words:

He is the lonely greatness of the world—
    (His eyes are dim)
His power it is holds up the Cross
    That holds up him.
He takes the sorrow of the threefold hour—
    (His eyelids close)
Round him and round, the wind—his Spirit—where
    It listeth blows.
And so the wounded greatness of the world
    In silence lies—
And death is shattered by the light from out
    Those darkened eyes.[4]

Love of Our Neighbor

I pray for the grace to look kindly upon my neighbor, never to judge.

Incline us, O God, to think humbly of ourselves,
to be saved only in the examination of our own conduct,
to consider our fellow creatures with kindness,
and to judge of all they say and do
with the charity which we would desire from them ourselves.[5]

Prayer for Our Global Family

May my heart expand to embrace the needs of all deprived of the basic necessities of life—they are all my sisters and brothers.

Creator Spirit, help us respond to our call to be members of one family.
Guide us to constant, peaceful concern
for sisters and brothers throughout the world.
Make us mindful of the needs of those
who must endure day by day the injustice of hunger and poverty.
Bless us all this Lenten season
that we may live in harmony and unity with others.
Renew our Christian commitment to the global family.[6]

A Prayer That Lent May Renew Us

Knowing that I am deeply loved by God, I ask forgiveness and renewal for "my shadow sides."

Dear God,
This season,
may I be reborn
washed clean
made new
forgiven
spectacularly loved.

Remind me who I am.
Forgive me for my shadow sides,
please heal my broken wings
that I might fly
with You. Amen.[7]

Words That Invite Reflection

Use these passages as an entry into deeper reflection and prayer with the spirit of this season of Lent.

Jesus' Temptations, Our Temptations

The Lenten liturgy begins with the temptations of Jesus in the desert, which deal with the three areas of instinctual need that every human being experiences in growing up. Jesus was tempted to satisfy his bodily hunger by seeking security in magic rather than in God; to jump off the pinnacle of the temple in order to make a name for himself as a wonder-worker; and to fall down and worship Satan in order to receive in exchange absolute power over the nations of the world. Security, esteem, power—these are three classic areas where temptation works on our false programs for happiness.[8]

A Reflection on the Works of Mercy

Knowing the commands of the Christ,
let this be our way of life:
let us feed the hungry
let us give the thirsty drink,
let us clothe the naked,
let us welcome strangers,
let us visit those in prison and the sick.
Then the judge of all will say even to us:

Come, you blessed of my Father,
inherit the realm prepared for you.[9]

Glimpsing the Mystery of Christ's Power

When all is said and done, what the world most needs from the church is not so much instruction about the nature of the mystery as a glimpse of the mystery itself operative in us. It already knows its own passion, and the vastness of the shipwreck of history; it waits for us to show it the power of Christ's passion and to lift our agony into his.

Adam and Jesus, you see—history's agent and history's Lord—have been in the same room all along. What a pity we have so often failed to introduce them.[10]

Christ Lives in His Mystical Body—Suffering, Dying, Rising Today

I have been disappointed and often disheartened, but with the passing of time I have come to realize that just because Christ does go on living on earth in His Mystical Body, the circumstances of His historical life must and will continue all through time too. Thus among His chosen apostles there always will be inconsistencies; there always will be those who, even after living a long time with Him, ask, "Who is the greatest in the Kingdom of Heaven?" and there will always be Pontius Pilates, condemning Him because to bow down before the humility and lowliness He stands for would cost them their prestige in the world . . . On the other hand, if His beauty seems at most almost hidden in what we see of Christians . . . it is also revealed vividly over and over again where one least expects it in what I call "Unconscious Christs," and in people who are not considered respectable by the world.[11]

CHAPTER TWELVE

Toward Easter: The Sacred Triduum

The Triduum, the three days from the evening of Holy Thursday to the evening of Easter Sunday, offers rich scripture texts, images, and symbols laden with meaning. *Pascha* is the "passing over" of the Lord, through death to life. As disciples and believers, we journey each year with him. To prepare to celebrate these high holy days, spend some time each day in prayerful communion with our suffering Savior, and recall that as a member of Christ's body, you too make the passage with him.

Because of the richness of the prayer texts, no additional introduction is provided. Cherish these texts; let them speak to your heart.

Holy Thursday Scriptures and Prayers

The Scriptures of Holy Thursday

Galatians 6:14

> May I never boast of anything except the cross of our Lord Jesus Christ, by which the world has been crucified to me, and I to the world.

John 13:12–15

> After he had washed their feet, had put on his robe, and had returned to the table, he said to them, "Do you know what I have done to you? You call me Teacher and Lord—and you are right, for that is what I am. So if I, your Lord and Teacher, have washed your feet, you also ought to wash one another's feet. For I have set you an example, that you also should do as I have done to you."

John 13:34–35

> I give you a new commandment, that you love one another. Just as I have loved you, you also should love one another. By this everyone will

know that you are my disciples, if you have love for one another.

1 Corinthians 11:23–26

For I received from the Lord what I also handed on to you, that the Lord Jesus on the night when he was betrayed took a loaf of bread, and when he had given thanks, he broke it and said, "This is my body that is for you. Do this in remembrance of me." In the same way he took the cup also, after supper, saying, "This cup is the new covenant in my blood. Do this, as often as you drink it, in remembrance of me." For as often as you eat this bread and drink the cup, you proclaim the Lord's death until he comes.

The Prayers of Holy Thursday

Acclamation to the Sacramental Christ

O sacrament most holy!
O sacrament divine!
All praise and all thanksgiving
Be every moment thine.

Desire for the Bread of Life

You satisfy the hungry heart
With gift of finest wheat;

Come give to us, O saving Lord,
The bread of life to eat.[1]

Jesus' Invitation to Us

Eat this bread, drink this cup,
come to me and never be hungry.
Eat this bread, drink this cup,
trust in me and you will not thirst.[2]

Eucharist, Memorial, and Promise

Lord Jesus Christ,
you gave us the Eucharist
as the memorial of your suffering and death.
May our worship of this sacrament of your body and blood
help us to know the salvation you won for us
and the peace of the kingdom
where you live with the Father and the Holy Spirit,
one God, for ever and ever. Amen.[3]

In Union with Christ

Lord Jesus Christ,
You experienced fully the weakness of our humanity
and were even betrayed by your friends.
By your blessed passion
be our comfort and protection
and strengthen us in our weakness.
You live and reign forever.[4]

Words That Invite Reflection

Use these passages as an entry into deeper reflection and prayer on the spirit of this day.

God's Desire for Communion with Us

God has enough of all good things
except one:
of communion with humans
God can never have enough.[5]

Where Love Is . . .

Where charity and love prevail, there God is ever found.
brought here together by Christ's love,
by love are we thus bound.[6]

Jesus' Gift of Himself

On the night of that Last Supper
Seated with his chosen band,
He, the paschal victim eating,
First fulfills the Law's command;
Then as food to his apostles
Gives himself with his own hand.[7]

Sing, My Tongue

A processional hymn at the end of the Holy Thursday liturgy.

Sing, my tongue, the song of triumph,
Tell the story far and wide;
Tell of dread and final battle,
Sing of Savior crucified;
How upon the cross a victim
Vanquishing in death he died.

He endured the nails, the spitting,
Vinegar and spear and reed;
From that holy body broken
Blood and water forth proceed:
Earth and stars and sky and ocean
By that flood from stain are freed.

Faithful Cross, above all other,
One and only noble tree,
None in foliage, none in blossom,
None in fruit your peer may be;
Sweet the wood and sweet the iron
And your load, most sweet is he.

Bend your boughs, O Tree of glory!
All your rigid branches, bend!
For a while the ancient temper
That your birth bestowed, suspend;
And the king of earth and heaven
Gently on your bosom tend.[8]

Good Friday Scriptures and Prayers

The Scriptures of Good Friday

Luke 23:46

Then Jesus, crying with a loud voice, said, "Father, into your hands I commend my spirit." Having said this, he breathed his last.

Hebrews 5:8–9

Although he was a Son, he learned obedience through what he suffered; and having been made perfect, he became the source of eternal salvation for all who obey him.

Isaiah 53:7–8, 10–11

He was oppressed, and he was afflicted, yet he did not open his mouth;
like a lamb that is led to the slaughter, and like a sheep that before its shearers is silent,
so he did not open his mouth.
By a perversion of justice he was taken away.

Yet it was the will of the Lord to crush him with pain. . . .
Out of his anguish he shall see light;
he shall find satisfaction through his knowledge.
The righteous one, my servant, shall make many

righteous,
and he shall bear their iniquities.

Galatians 2:19–21

I have been crucified with Christ; and it is no longer I who live, but it is Christ who lives in me. And the life I now live in the flesh I live by faith in the Son of God, who loved me and gave himself for me.

The Prayers of Good Friday

Acclamations to Christ Crucified and Victorious

Holy is God!
Holy and strong!
Holy immortal One,
have mercy on us![9]

We adore you, O Christ, and we bless you!
By your holy cross you have redeemed the world.[10]

To Jesus, Man of Sorrows

Holy Redeemer,
a man of sorrows and acquainted with grief,
you were led to the slaughter like a lamb
but you did not open your mouth against them.
By this suffering, release us from sin

and rouse us from the sleep of death,
O Savior of the world,
living and reigning, now and for ever.
Amen.[11]

Surrender

Into your hands, God,
This solitude,
Into your hands, God,
This emptiness.
Into your hands, God,
This loneliness.
Into your hands—
This all.
Into your hands, O God,
This grief.
Into your hands—
This sleeping fear.

Into your hands, O God—
What is left,
What is left
Of me.[12]

Jesus, Weak and Betrayed

Lord Jesus Christ,
You experienced fully the weakness of our humanity
and were even betrayed by your friends.
By your blessed passion

be our comfort and protection
and strengthen us in our weakness.
You live and reign for ever. Amen.[13]

Hear Us and Have Mercy

Lord Jesus, who was betrayed by the kiss of Judas Iscariot in the Garden of Gethsemane:
Hear us and have mercy.

Lord Jesus, who was condemned to death for us by Pontius Pilate:
Hear us and have mercy.

Lord Jesus, who was flogged for us at the pillar:
Hear us and have mercy.

Lord Jesus, who was crowned with thorns for us, mocked and insulted:
Hear us and have mercy.

Lord Jesus, who carried the cross to Golgotha for us:
Hear us and have mercy.

Lord Jesus, who was crucified for us:
Hear us and have mercy.

Lord Jesus, who was buried for us in the tomb:
Hear us and have mercy.

Lord Jesus, who rose for us on the third day:
Hear us and have mercy.

Lord Jesus, who flooded the world with the light of the Holy Spirit:
Hear us and have mercy.[14]

Words That Invite Reflection

Use these passages as an entry into deeper reflection and prayer on the spirit of this day.

In Company with Mary, at the Foot of the Cross

At the cross her station keeping
stood the mournful Mother weeping
Close to Jesus to the last.

In the Passion of my Maker
Be my sinful soul partaker,
May I with her bear my part.

Of his passion bear the token
In a spirit bowed and broken
Bear his death within my heart.

May his wounds both wound and heal me,
He enkindle, cleanse, and heal me,
Be his cross my hope and stay.[15]

Holy the Cross!

This ancient text images the Cross of Jesus Christ as the life-giving tree. As you savor its poetry, pray for a deepening sense of gratitude for Christ's gift of himself so that we may make the passage with him into fuller life.

> O tree of beauty, tree most fair,
> Ordained those holy limbs to bear:
> Gone is your shame, each crimsoned bough
> Proclaims the King of glory now.
>
> Blest tree, whose chosen branches bore
> The wealth that did the world, restore,
> The price of humankind to pay
> And spoil the spoiler of this prey.

The Sign of the Cross

> On the cross Christ redeemed humankind. By the cross he sanctifies us, to the last shred and fiber of our being. We make the Sign of the Cross before we pray to collect and compose ourselves and to fix our minds and hearts and wills upon God. We make it when we finish praying in order that we may hold fast the gift we have received from God. In temptations we sign ourselves to be strengthened; in dangers, to be protected. The cross is signed upon us in blessings in order that the fullness of God's life may flow into the soul and fructify and sanctify us wholly.[16]

Christ Carried Us on the Cross

It is Christ in us who can say with absolute trust in the hour of death; "Under me are the everlasting arms." It is Christ in us, Christ whose death we are dying, who can say with absolute faith, both for ourselves and for those whom we love: Into Thy hands, O Lord . . ."

That is why Christ would not, could not, come down from the cross. On the cross He carried us all through the darkness of death to the light, through the chill of death to the warmth, through the fear of death to the love of God. It is with His heart that we love the Father in the hour of death, because He has given His heart. He has given us our Heaven.[17]

Easter Scriptures and Prayers

The Scriptures of Easter

Psalm 104:24–26, 33–35

O Lord, how manifold are your works!
In wisdom you have made them all;
the earth is full of your creatures.
Yonder is the sea, great and wide,
creeping things innumerable are there,
living things both small and great.
There go the ships,

and Leviathan that you formed to sport in it.
I will sing to the Lord as long as I live;
I will sing praise to my God while I have being.
May my meditation be pleasing to him,
for I rejoice in the Lord.

Psalm 77: 11–13, 16–20

Bless the Lord, O my soul.
Praise the Lord!

I will call to mind the deeds of the Lord;
I will remember your wonders of old.
I will meditate on all your work,
and muse on your mighty deeds.
Your way, O God, is holy.

When the waters saw you, O God,
when the waters saw you, they were afraid;
the very deep trembled.
The clouds poured out water;
the skies thundered;
your arrows flashed on every side.
The crash of your thunder was in the whirlwind;
your lightnings lit up the world;
the earth trembled and shook.
Your way was through the sea,
your path, through the mighty waters;
yet your footprints were unseen.
You led your people like a flock
by the hand of Moses and Aaron.

Psalm 145: 10–13, 15–16

All your works shall give thanks to you, O Lord,
and all your faithful shall bless you.
They shall speak of the glory of your kingdom,
and tell of your power,
to make known to all people your mighty deeds,
and the glorious splendor of your kingdom.
Your kingdom is an everlasting kingdom
and your dominion endures throughout all
generations.

The eyes of all look to you,
and you give them their food in due season.
You open your hand,
satisfying the desire of every living thing.

Isaiah 60:19

Nor the brightness of the moon shine upon you at
night;
The Lord shall be your light forever, your God shall be
your glory.

John 20:16–18

Jesus said to her, "Mary!" She turned and said to him in Hebrew, "Rabbouni!" (which means Teacher). Jesus said to her ". . . go to my brothers and say to them, 'I am ascending to my Father and your Father, to my God and your God.'"

Mary Magdalene went and announced to the disciples, "I have seen the Lord"; and she told them that he had said these things to her.

Luke 24:1–5

But on the first day of the week, at early dawn, the women came to the tomb, taking the spices that they had prepared. They found the stone rolled away from the tomb, but when they went in, they did not find the body. While they were perplexed about this, suddenly two men in dazzling clothes stood beside them. The women were terrified and bowed their faces to the ground, but the men said to them, "Why do you look for the living among the dead? He is not here, but has risen."

Luke 24:30–33

When [Jesus] was at the table with them [the Emmaus disciples], he took bread, blessed and broke it, and gave it to them. Then their eyes were opened, and they recognized him; and he vanished from their sight. They said to each other, "Were not our hearts burning within us while he was talking to us on the road, while he was opening the scriptures to us?

The Prayers of Easter

Thanksgiving for the Easter Mystery

Prayed at Easter Vespers.

Blessed are you, O Lord our God.
In every age you have written our history in water.
From the chaos of the seas you brought forth our world.
From the midst of the Red Sea you gave birth to a people.
through the Jordan you brought Israel to a promised land
and sent forth your Son to be the anointed
who would proclaim the good news of your kingdom.
In these days you have again recreated and formed us.
In the memorial of Christ's death and rising
new sons and daughters have been born
from the font, the womb of your church.
Keep alive in all of us the joy of this season
that always and everywhere the Easter alleluia
may arise as a hymn of glory to your name.
All power and glory be to you
through Jesus our risen Lord
in the life-giving love of the Holy Spirit
this eventide and forever and ever. Amen.[18]

An Easter Prayer for the Church

Abba, dear Father,
your love is eternal, your fidelity unceasing.

By the love you showed your only Son,
when you saved him from the grave,
stretch out your hand to save the church
that struggles to do your holy will,
through the same Christ our Lord.
Amen.[19]

An Emmaus Prayer

Remain with us, Lord Jesus,
You who were the guest at Emmaus;
Throughout the watches of the night,
Resurrected, you lead us.

Taking bread, you broke it,
Then our eyes recognized you,
The flickering flame in our heart
Foretells our true happiness.

The time is short, our days are fleeting.
But you prepare your house,
You give a meaning to our desires,
A future to our labors.

You the first of the pilgrims,
The star of the last morning,
Awake in us by your love
A great hope in your return.[20]

Words That Invite Reflection

Use these passages as an entry into deeper reflection on the spirit of the season of Easter.

The Paschal Candle, Christ our Light

> Throughout Easter's fifty days the paschal candle stands . . . Lit as the first act of the community's paschal watch, this mighty pillar of light remains in place for the duration of the fifty days enabling the faithful to see, to recognize, to find their way. It is the light of Christ revealing the love of the Father, and the power of the Spirit in whom humanity is born from above.[21]

Recognizing Jesus

> The price of recognizing Jesus is always the same; our idea of him, of the church, of the spiritual journey, of God himself has to be shattered. To see with the eyes of faith we must be free of our culturally conditioned mindsets. When we let go of our private and limited vision, he who has been hidden from us by our pre-packaged values and preconceived ideas causes the scales to fall from our eyes. He was there all the time. Now at last we perceive his presence. With the transformed vision of faith, we return to the humdrum routines and duties of daily life, but now, like Mary Magdalene, we recognize God giving himself to us in everyone and in everything.[22]

Easter, a Return to Our Baptism

Even though we are baptized, what we constantly lose and betray is precisely that which we received at baptism. Therefore Easter is our return every year to our own baptism, whereas Lent is our preparation for that return—the slow and sustained effort to perform, at the end, our own "passage" or "pascha" into the new life in Christ. . . . Each year Lent and Easter are, once again, the rediscovery and the recovery by us of what we were made through our own baptismal death and resurrection.[23]

Christ: Image and Reality

He is the Pascha of our salvation.
It is he who, in many, endured many things:
    It is he that was in Abel murdered
    and in Isaac bound,
    and in Jacob exiled,
and in Joseph sold,
and in Moses exposed,
and in the lamb slain
and in David persecuted,
and in the prophets dishonored.
It is he that was enfleshed in a virgin,
that was hanged on a tree,
that was buried in the earth,
that was raised from the dead,
that was taken up to the heights of the heavens.
He is the lamb being slain;

he is the lamb that is speechless;
he is the one born from Mary the lovely ewe-lamb;
he is the one taken *from the flock,*
and dragged *to slaughter,*
and sacrificed *at evening,*
and buried *at night;*
who on the tree was *not broken,*
in the earth was not dissolved,
who arose from the dead,
and raised up humankind from the grave below.[24]

Christ, My Personal Savior
The risen, living Christ
Calls me by name;
Comes to the loneliness within me;
Heals that which is wounded in me;
Comforts that which grieves in me;
Seeks for that which is lost within me;
Releases me from that which has dominion over me;
Cleanses me of that which does not belong to me;
Renews that which feels drained within me;
Awakens that which is asleep in me;
Names that which is formless within me;
Empowers that which is newborn within me;
Consecrates and guides that which is strong within me;
Restores me to this world which needs me;
Reaches out in endless love to others through me.[25]

Let Him Easter in Us . . .

Let him Easter in us
be a dayspring to the dimness in us,
be a crimson-cresseted East.[26]

Gifts Remain with Us

These many beautiful days cannot be lived again. But they are compounded in my own flesh and spirit and I take them in full measure with me toward whatever lies ahead.[27]

CHAPTER THIRTEEN

Pentecost

The Scriptures of Pentecost

John 16:12–13

I still have many things to say to you, but you cannot bear them now. When the Spirit of truth comes, he will guide you into all the truth; for he will not speak on his own, but will speak whatever he hears, and he will declare to you the things that are to come.

Acts 2:1–2, 4

> When the day of Pentecost had come, they were all together in one place. And suddenly from heaven there came a sound like the rush of a violent wind, and it filled the entire house where they were sitting. . . . All of them were filled with the Holy Spirit and began to speak in other languages, as the Spirit gave them ability.

Romans 5:5

> God's love has been poured into our hearts through the Holy Spirit that has been given to us.

Romans 8:26–27

> Likewise the Spirit helps us in our weakness; for we do not know how to pray as we ought, but that very Spirit intercedes with sighs too deep for words. And God, who searches the heart, knows what is the mind of the Spirit, because the Spirit intercedes for the saints according to the will of God.

The Prayers of Pentecost

Come, Holy Spirit

As the Spirit acted in that first Pentecost, so do we pray the Spirit to act again in us.

Come, Holy Spirit, fill the hearts of your faithful and kindle in them the fire of your love.
Send forth your Spirit, O Lord, and renew the face of the earth!

O God, on the first Pentecost
you instructed the hearts of those who believed in you
by the light of the Holy Spirit:
under the inspiration of the same Spirit,
give us a taste for what is right and true
and a continuing sense of the Spirit's joy-bringing presence and power,
through Jesus Christ our Lord.
Amen.[1]

The Way of True Discipleship

May God send the spirit to touch our hearts and to lead us in the way of true discipleship . . .

Holy God,
source of light and wisdom,
give us hearts that seek the truth.
In our comings and goings,
show us the way of true discipleship.
Touch our hearts and fire our world
with your own Spirit.
We pray in Jesus' name. Amen.[2]

Come, Spirit of God . . .

May we be made new by the living Spirit of God.

Spirit of God, find a home in us.
Spirit of God, animate us.
Spirit of God, create new hearts in us.[3]

Weave Us into One

Using the image of the Spirit as the great weaver, we pray to be woven into one family.

Spirit of love, who moves with creation,
drawing the threads to color and design,
life into life, you knit our true salvation:
Come, work with us, and weave us into one.
Though we have frayed the fabric of your making,
tearing away from all that you intend,
yet to be whole, humanity is aching:
Come, work with us, and weave us into one.
Great loom of God, where history is woven,
you are the frame that holds us to the truth,
Christ is the theme, the pattern you have given:
Come, work with us, and weave us into one.[4]

Prayer to the Holy Spirit

A prayer for transformation, that we may become "the warm humanity of Christ."

Come down upon us,
Spirit of God,
spirit of wisdom
and peace and joy;
come as a great wind blowing;
sweep our minds with a storm of light.
Be in us as bright fire burning;
forge our wills to shining swords
in the flame.
Purify our hearts
in the crucible
of the fire of love.
Change our tepid nature
into the warm humanity
of Christ,
as he changed water into wine.
Be in us a stream of life,
as wine in the living vine.[5]

Prayer to the Holy Spirit (from Pope John XXIII)

In the following two prayers from Pope John XXIII, I pray that the work of Jesus will continue and be completed in us.

O Holy Spirit, Paraclete,
perfect in us the work begun by Jesus;
enable us to continue to pray fervently
in the name of the whole world.
Hasten in every one of us
the growth of a deep interior life;
give vigor to our apostolate
so that it may reach all peoples,

all redeemed by the blood of Christ
and all belonging to him . . .
Let no earthly bond prevent us from honoring our vocation,
no cowardly considerations disturb the claims of justice,
no meanness confine the immensity of charity
within the narrow bounds of petty selfishness.
let everything in us be on a grand scale:
the search for truth, and the devotion to it;
and readiness for self-sacrifice, even to the cross and death;
and may everything finally
be according to your will,
O Holy Spirit of love,
which the Father and the Son desired
to be poured out over the Church and its institutions,
over each and every human soul and over nations.[6]

O divine Spirit . . . renew in our own days your miracles as of a second Pentecost.[7]

Sequence of Pentecost

Holy Spirit, font of light,
focus of God's glory bright,
shed on us a shining ray.
Father of the fatherless,
giver of gifts limitless,
come and touch our hearts today.

Source of strength and sure relief,
comforter in time of grief,
enter in and be our guest.
On our journey grant us aid,
freshening breeze and cooling shade,
in our labor inward rest.

Enter each aspiring heart,
occupy its inmost part
with your dazzling purity.
All that gives to human worth,
all that benefits the earth,
you bring to maturity.

With your soft refreshing rains
break our drought, remove our stains;
bind up all our injuries.
Shake with rushing wind our will;
melt with fire our icy chill;
bring to light our perjuries.

As your promise we believe
make us ready to receive
gifts from your unbounded store.
Grant enabling energy,
courage in adversity,
joys that last for evermore.[8]

Words That Invite Reflection

Use these passages as an entry into deeper reflection and prayer on the spirit of the season of Pentecost.

God's Grandeur

The world is charged with the grandeur of God.
It will flame out, like shining from shook foil;
It gathers to a greatness, like the ooze of oil
Crushed. Why do men then now not reck his rod?
Generations have trod, have trod, have trod;
And all is seared with trade; bleared, smeared with toil;
And wears man's smudge and shares man's smell: the soil
Is bare now, nor can foot feel, being shod.

And for all this, nature is never spent;
There lives the dearest freshness deep down things;
And though the last lights off the black West went
Oh, morning, at the brown brink eastward, springs—
Because the Holy Ghost over the bent
World broods with warm breast and with ah! bright wings.[9]

Sacred Chrism, the "Aroma of Christ"

The sign of Christ is traced on the part of the body that is most visible to anyone who meets us. How can anyone observe Mother Teresa at work serving the starving children of Calcutta and not smell something of this strong and wholesome fragrance, this "aroma of Christ"? This woman has translated into action what the bishop meant when on the day of her confirmation he laid his hand on her head and anointed her forehead so that she might confess her faith and bear witness to it.[10]

The Church's Greatest Need

What does the Church need?
The Church needs the Spirit
the Holy Spirit.
He it is who animates and sanctifies the Church.
He is her divine breath,
the wind in her sails,
the principle of her unity,
the inner source of her light and strength.
He is her support and consoler,
her source of charisms and songs,
her peace and her joy
her pledge and prelude to blessed and eternal life.

The Church needs her perennial Pentecost.
She needs fire in her heart,
words on her lips,
prophecy in her outlook.
She needs to be the temple of the Holy Spirit.

In the empty silence of the modern world
the Church needs to feel rising
from the depths of her inmost personality,
a weeping, a poem, a prayer, a hymn—
the praying voice of the Spirit,
who prays in us and for us
"with sighs too deep for words."

She needs to listen in silence
and in an attitude of total availability
to the voice of the Spirit
who teaches "every truth."

The Church needs to feel flowing
through all her human faculties
a wave of love,
that love which is called forth
and poured into our hearts
"by the Holy Spirit who has been given to us."

This is what the Church needs;
she needs the Holy Spirit!
The Holy Spirit in us,
in each of us,
and in all of us together,
in us who are the Church.

So let all of us ever say to him,
"Come."[11]

Acknowledgments

The publisher gratefully acknowledges the permission granted to use the following sources from which portions of this book were compiled.

Unless otherwise acknowledged, all other prayers are composed by the author. Every effort has been made to give proper acknowledgment to authors and copyright holders of the texts herein. If any omissions or errors have been made please notify the publisher who will correct it in future editions.

Alleluia Press, Allendale, NJ. *Byzantine Daily Worship* by Joseph Raya and Jose De Vinck, © 1969 for "Prayer of Thanksgiving at Easter Vespers."

ACTA Publications, Chicago, IL. "Prayer at the End of Day" and "Lunch Blessing" from *A Contemporary Celtic Prayer Book* by William John Fitzgerald © 1998. Used with permission. www.actapublications.com.

Robert F. Capon, *An Offering of Uncles*. Permission granted by the author.

Church Publishing for stanza from "Creator of the Stars of Night," from *The Hymnal 1982*, © 1985 the Church Pension Fund. All rights reserved. Used by permission of Church Publishing Incorporated, New York, NY.

Claretian Publications, Chicago, IL. "Prayer to Dorothy Day," reprinted with permission from Claretian Publications, 205 W. Monroe St., Chicago, IL, 60606, 312-236-7782, www.claretianpubs.org.

Continuum International Publishing Group. *The Mystery of Christ: The Liturgy as Spiritual Experience* by Thomas Keating, © 2000 for selected seasonal excerpts. Reprinted with the permission of the publisher.

Congregation of St. Joseph, Los Angeles Province, for use of an unpublished prayer by Sisters Clara Dunn and Judy Lovehik.

Dominican Sisters, Summit, NJ, for use of a poem by Madeleine Caron Rock.

GIA Publications, Chicago, IL, for a verse from "Eat This Bread," adapted by Robert J. Batastini and the Taizé Community.

Graymoor Ecumenical and Interreligious Institute, for "Prayer for the Unity of the Church."

J. Frank Henderson, for use of texts from *A Prayer Book for Remembering the Women*.

ICS Publications. *Elizabeth of the Trinity. The Complete Works., Vol. I*. Translated by Sr. Aletheia Kane, O.C.D., © 1984, Washington Province of the Discalced Carmelites, Inc. ICS Publications, 2131 Lincoln Road, N.E. Washington D.C., 20002-1199, www.icspublications.org.

Institute of Jesuit Resources, St. Louis, MO. *Hearts on Fire: Praying with the Jesuits*, Michael Harter, S.J., ed., for "Prayer for the Grace to Age Well," and prayer of Teilhard de Chardin, "When the Signs of Age Begin to Mark My Body," © 1993, 2005. Used with permission. © The Institute of Jesuit Sources, St. Louis MO. All rights reserved.

Liturgical Press, Collegeville, MN. *Psalter for the Christian People,* Gail Ramshaw and Gordon Lathrop, eds., © 2002 for "Psalm 33" and "Psalm 100."

Liturgy Training Publications, Chicago, IL. *A Seasonal Book of Hours* by William G. Storey, © 2001 for "Lord, Jesus Christ"; "Abba, Loving Father"; "Creator and Redeemer"; "Holy Redeemer"; "Lord Jesus, Who Was Betrayed"; and "Abba, Dear Father." Archdiocese of Chicago, Liturgy Training Publications. 1-800-933-1800. www.LTP.org. All rights reserved. Used with permission.

Maryknoll Sisters Center, Maryknoll, NY, for prayer texts by Sister Joan Metzner, "Here We Are God, a Planet at Prayer" and "I Believe There Is Someone Waiting for Me."

Morehouse Publishing Company, New York. *All Desires Known*, © 2006 for Janet Morley's "Sing Out My Soul."

Sisters of Notre Dame de Namur, Cincinnati, OH, for two unpublished texts by Sister Dorothy Stang, S.N.D. de N.

Orbis Publishing Co., Maryknoll, NY. *Theology Brewed in an African Pot* by Agbonkhianmeghe E. Orobator, © 2008. Used with permission.

Oxford University Press. *The Poems of Gerard Manley Hopkins,* Robert Bridges, ed., © 1935, for works in copyright by Permission of Oxford University Press on behalf of the British Province of the Society of Jesus.

The Oxford Book of Prayer, George Appleton, ed., © 1985 for Irish Rune, eighth century.

The Wisdom of the Saints: An Anthology, Jill Haak Adels, ed., © 1987 for quotation by Teresa of Avila.

Paulist Press, Mahwah, NJ. Excerpts from *All Shall Be Well: The Spirituality of Julian of Norwich for Today*, by Robert Llewelyn. Copyright © 1982 by Robert Llewelyn. Paulist Press, Inc., New York, Mahwah, NJ. Reprinted by permission of Paulist Press, Inc. www.paulistpress.com.

Excerpts from *Julian of Norwich: Showings*, translated and introduced by Edmund Colledge, O.S.A., and James Walsh, S.J. Copyright © 1978 The Missionary Society of St. Paul the Apostle in the State of New York. Paulist Press, Inc., New York, Mahwah, NJ. Reprinted by permission of Paulist Press, Inc. www.paulistpress.com.

Excerpts from *Mechtild of Magdeburg:The Flowing Light of the Godhead*, translated and introduced by Frank Tobin. Copyright © 1998 by Fran Tobin. Paulist Press, Inc., New York, Mahwah, NJ. Reprinted by permission of Paulist Press, Inc. www.paulistpress.com.

Excerpts from *The Pattern of Our Days. Worship in the Celtic Tradition from the Iona Community*, copyright © 1996 by The Authors. Paulist Press, Inc., New York, Mahwah, NJ. Reprinted by permission of Paulist Press, Inc. www.paulistpress.com.

Red Cloud Indian School, Pine Ridge, South Dakota, for use of an unpublished prayer from the Native American Tradition. Used with permission of the Director.

Salesian Missions, New Rochelle, NY, for an unpublished prayer by Samuel Pugh: "O God, When I Have Food, Help Me to Remember." Used with permission.

Sheed and Ward, New York. *Psalms of a Laywoman* by Edwina Gately, © 1999 for "Silent God" and "Surrender." Used with permission.

SPCK Publishing & Sheldon Press, London. *Bread of Tomorrow: Praying with the World's Poor* by Janet Morley, Copyright © 1992 for "For All the Saints."

Brother David Steindl-Rast, O.S.B., for "Prayer for Unity" on http://www.gratefulnessorg/poetry/UnityPrayer.htm.

Ateliers et Presses de Taizé, Communauté de Taizé, Taizé, France, for use of prayer by Brother Roger Schutz, "O Christ, You Take Upon Yourself all Our Burdens."

United Reformed Church. *Prayer Handbook 1988 Encounters*, for "Lord Jesus, Rabbi, Teacher . . ." by Kate Compston.

University of California Press. Excerpt from *The Catholic Imagination* by Andrew Greeley, © 2000 by the Regents of the University of California. Published by the University of California Press.

Upper Room Books, United Methodist Church, Nashville, TN. Excerpt reprinted from *Prayer, Fear and Our Powers: Finding Our Healing, Release, and Growth in Christ* by Flora Slosson Wuellner. © 1989 by The Upper Room®. Used by permission from Upper Room Books®.

World Library Publications, Chicago, IL. Excerpt from "Where Charity and Love Prevail," translation by Omer Westendorf. Text copyright © 1960, World Library Publications, wlpmusic.com. All Rights Reserved. Used with permission.

Notes

Part One: An Invitation to Pray

1. Frederick Buechner, *Now and Then: A Memoir of Vocation* (San Francisco: HarperOne, 1991), 87.

2. Anne Morrow Lindbergh, *Gift from the Sea* (New York: Pantheon Books, 1975), 50.

Chapter One

1. "Te Deum," in *Lord Hear Our Prayer*, revised edition, ed. William G. Storey and Thomas McNally, C.S.C. (Notre Dame, IN: Ave Maria Press, 2000), 20–22.

2. *Prayer without Borders: Celebrating Global Wisdom*, ed. Barbara Ballenger (Baltimore, MD: Catholic Relief Services, 2005), 59.

3. Dorothy Stang, S.N.D. de N., "Thanks for My Life," (unpublished), (Cincinnati, OH: Archives of the Sisters of Notre Dame de Namur)

4. Unknown author, "This Earthly Fellowship," in *God Has No Religion: Blending Traditions for Prayer*, ed. Frances Sheridan Goulart (Notre Dame, IN: Sorin Books, 2005), 160.

5. Elizabeth of the Trinity, Elizabeth of the Trinity: *The Complete Works, Volume One*, trans. Sister Aletheia Kane, O.C.D. (Washington, DC: ICS Publications, 1984), 183.

6. Teresa of Avila.

7. Julian of Norwich, *Showings: The Classics of Western Spirituality*, trans. Edmund Colledge, O.S.A., and James Walsh, S.J. (Mahwah, NJ: Paulist Press, 1978), 184.

8. *Mechthild of Magdeburg: The Flowing Light of the Godhead*, trans. Frank Tobin (Mahwah, NJ: Paulist Press, 1998), xxx.

9. Ibid., 59.

10. Gertrud Mueller Nelson and Christopher Witt, *Pocket Prayers* (New York: Image Books, 1995), 25–26.

11. Edwina Gateley, *Psalms of a Laywoman* (Franklin, WI: Sheed & Ward, 1998), 50.

12. Dietrich Bonhoeffer in Goulart, *God Has No Religion*, 66.

13. Ignatius of Loyola, "Prayer against Depression," *Catholic Online*, http://www.catholic.org/prayers/prayer.php?p=616.

14. Bernhard Häring, C.Ss.R., *Prayer: The Integration of Faith and Life* (Notre Dame, IN: Fides Publishers, 1975), 30.

15. John Henry Newman, "The Pillar of the Cloud," in Goulart, *God Has No Religion*, 42.

16. Pedro Arupe, S.J.

17. Julian of Norwich, *Showings*, 249.

18. Julian of Norwich, *Showings*, 151.

19. Meister Eckhart.

20. Teresa of Avila.

21. Julian of Norwich, *Showings*, 221.

Chapter Two

1. Elizabeth Barrett Browning, "Aurora Leigh."

2. Francis of Assisi, "Canticle of Brother Sun and Sister Moon," in Storey

and McNally, *Lord Hear Our Prayer,* 38–40.

3. UN Environmental Sabbath Program. The UNESP no longer exists, but encourages dissemination of its materials.

4. Joan Metzner, M.M. Permission for use granted by the Maryknoll Sisters, Maryknoll, New York.

5. Edward Hays, *Prayers for a Planetary Pilgrim* (Notre Dame, IN: Ave Maria Press, 2008), 11.

6. Ibid., 168.

7. Red Cloud Indian School, Pine Ridge, North Dakota, 1989.

8. UN Environmental Sabbath Program.

9. Caryll Houselander, *The Reed of God* (Notre Dame, IN: Christian Classics, 2006), 91–92.

10. *Hildegard of Bingen: Devotions, Prayers, & Living Wisdom*, ed. Mirabai Starr (Boulder, CO: Sounds True, Inc.), 79.

11. UN Environmental Sabbath Program.

12. *Anne Frank: The Diary of a Young Girl*, trans. B.M. Mooyaart-Doubleday (New York: Pocketbooks/Simon and Shuester, 1952), 142–143.

13. Archibald MacLeish, "Riders on Earth Together, Brothers in Eternal Cold," *New York Times*, December 25, 1968.

14. Guru Angad in *Earth Prayers from around the World: 365 Prayers, Poems, and Invocations for Honoring the Earth*, eds. Elizabeth Roberts and Elias Amidon (San Francisco: HarperOne: 1991), 363.

15. Hildegard of Bingen in Roberts and Amidon, *Earth Prayers*, 69.

16. Joseph P. Allen, interview by Frank White, *The Overview Effect: Space Exploration and Human Evolution*, (Reston, VA: AAIA, 1998), 215.

17. St. Augustine.

Chapter Three

1. Ballenger, *Prayer without Borders*, 17.

2. Nelson and Witt, *Pocket Prayers*, 84–85.

3. Ibid., 87–88.

4. Marie Schwan, C.S.J. (unpublished prayer).

5. Fran Hopkins, from the website *Families.com.* Last modified April 19, 2006. http://single-parenting.families.com/blog/refresh-your-spirit-prayers-for-single-p.

6. Agbonkhianmeghe E. Orobator, *Theology Brewed in an African Pot* (Maryknoll, NY: Orbis Books, 2008), 109.

7. Nelson and Witt, *Pocket Prayers*, 108–09.

8. Orobator, *Theology Brewed in an African Pot*, 107–08.

9. From the website *My Forever Child.* http://www.myforeverchild.com/store/WsDefault.asp?Cat=Fertility-PregnancyJewelry&Sub=80&isThumbs=Yes&Thumbs=100.

10. *Bread for Tomorrow: Prayers for the Church Year*, ed. Janet Morley (Maryknoll, NY: Orbis Books, 1992), 135.

11. Nelson and Witt, *Pocket Prayers*, 106–07.

12. Caryll Houselander, *The Reed of God* (Notre Dame, IN: Christian Classics, 2006), 62–63.

13. Andrew M. Greeley, *The Jesus Myth* (Garden City, NY: Doubleday, 1971), 48.

14. Julian of Norwich, *Showings,* 296–97.

15. John of the Cross.

16. Helen Weaver in Roberts and Amidon, *Earth Prayers,* 115.

17. From Women's World Day of Prayer, 1993.

18. Mary Kathleen Speegle Schmitt, "Heart of Compassion," in Goulart, *God Has No Religion,* 144.

19. World Council of Churches, Vancouver Assembly, 1983, in Goulart, *God Has No Religion*, 148.

20. Miriam Teichner, "Prayer Awareness," in *Inspirational Words of Wisdom*, http://www.inspirationalwordsofwisdom.com/prayer-awareness.html.

21. "Prayer to Dorothy Day," from the website *Justpeace.org.* http://www.justpeace.org/saintprayers.htm#Prayers%20to%20Saints%20for%20Justice%20and%20Peace.

22. Samuel F. Pugh, "A Thanksgiving Prayer," *Appleseeds,* http://www.appleseeds.org/thankgv5.htm.

23. Ballenger, *Prayer without Borders*, 13.

24. Ibid., 18.

25. "Respect Life," *eCatholic 2000,* http://www.ecatholic2000.com/pray/prayer21.shtml.

26. Helen Prejean, C.S.J., "A Prayer to Abolish the Death Penalty."

27. Ballenger, *Prayer without Borders*, 68.

28. Mary Lou Kownacki, O.S.B., "Prayer for the Decade of Nonviolence."

29. Mary Lou Kownacki, O.S.B., "Prayer for Peace and Justice."

30. William Laud, "For the Church," in Storey and McNally, *Lord Hear Our Prayer,* 61–62.

31. "For the Unity of the Church," Graymoor Ecumenical and Interreligious Institute, Garrison, NY, http://www.geii.org.

32. Liturgy Training Publications, Chicago, IL, from a prayer card.

33. Teresa of Avila.

34. Clare Dunn, C.S.J., and Judy Lovehik, C.S.J., from a prayer card.

35. Christopher Fry, "A Sleep of Prisoners," http://www.gratefulness.org/poetry/sleep_of_prisoners.htm.

36. Bl. Mother Teresa of Calcutta.

37. Irish Rune, Eighth Century, in *The Oxford Book of Prayer*, ed. George Appleton (New York, Oxford University Press USA, 2002), 171.

38. Unknown author. A prayer from the Peace Mass, January 1, 2009, St. Peter in Chains Cathedral, Cincinnati, OH.

39. Mahatma Gandhi.

40. Bl. Mother Teresa.

41. Margaret Mead.

Chapter Four

1. Roger Schutz, "Easter" from the Taizé community. Used with permission.

2. Prayer panels at Coventry Cathedral, England.

3. "Visigothic Liturgy," in Storey and McNally, *Lord Hear Our Prayer,* 57–58.

4. Julian of Norwich, *Showings,* 151.

5. Sr. Teresita Weind S.N.D. de N., "Prayer for Healing," http://www.notredameonline.org/SrDorothyStang.html.

6. Monica Furlong, "Jesus Who Never Grew Old," in *Soul Weaving: A Gathering of Women's Prayers,* ed. Lyn Klug (Minneapolis: Augsburg Fortress, 1996), 100.

7. Teresa of Avila.

8. Ibid.

9. Jane de Chantal.

10. Dorothea Dix.

11. Barb McCartney, "God of Inner Knowing," (unpublished prayer).

12. Teresa of Avila in *WomanPrayers, Prayers by Women from Throughout History and Around the World,* ed. Mary Ford-Grabowsky (San Francisco: HarperOne, 2003), 109–110.

13. The Iona Community, *The Pattern of Our Days: Worship in the Celtic Tradition*, ed. Kathy Galloway (Mahwah, NJ: Paulist Press, 1996), 99.

14. Ibid, 134.

15. Dorothy Stang S.N.D. de N., "A Prayer of Self-offering," (unpublished), (Cincinnati, OH: Archives of the Sisters of Notre Dame de Namur).

16. The Iona Community, in *The Pattern of Our Days*, 158.

17. Monica Furlong, "Dear God, It Is So Hard," in Ford-Grabowski, *WomanPrayers*, 125.

18. Robert Llwelyn, *All Shall Be Well: The Spirituality of Julian of Norwich for Today* (Mahwah, NJ: Paulist Press, 1982), 136.

19. Ranier Maria Rilke, *Letters to a Young Poet*, trans. M.D. Herter Norton (New York: W.W. Norton, 1993).

20. Adapted from a prayer for the first ordination of Anglican women in Ford-Grabowski, *WomanPrayers*, 99.

21. Julian of Norwich, *Revelation of Love*, trans. John Skinner (New York: Image Books, 1997), 77, 80–81.

22. Barbara Searle, "Our Lives, a Wreath" (unpublished poem).

23. Teresa of Avila.

24. Frederick Buechner, *Wishful Thinking: A Seeker's ABC* (San Francisco: HarperOne, 1993), 119.

25. Elizabeth Kubler-Ross.

26. Pierre Teilhard de Chardin, "Prayer for the Grace to Age Well," in *Hearts on Fire: Praying with Jesuits,* ed. Michael G. Harter (Chicago: Loyola Press, 2005), 178.

27. Madeleine L'Engle, *The Weather of the Heart* (Wheaton, IL: Shaw Publishers, 2000), 70.

28. Teresa of Avila, "Death," in *The Wisdom of the Saints,* ed. Jill Haak Adels (New York: Oxford University Press, 1987), 197.

29. "Just a Closer Walk with Thee," in *Lead Me, Guide Me*, (Chicago: GIA Publications), #156.

30. African American Spiritual, in *Lead me, Guide Me*, #319.

31. Joan Metzner, M.M., "Homecoming," http://www.nhlcyberfamily.org/inspiration/poems.htm.

32. Sister Marie of the Holy Spirit, Carmelite of Chalons.

33. From a funeral homily by Gerard Sloyan, July 11, 1979.

34. Monika Hellwig, *The Meaning of the Sacraments* (Dayton, OH: Pflaum/Standard, 1972), 94.

Chapter Five

1. I am grateful for insights drawn from Barbara E. Bowe's *Biblical*

Foundations of Spirituality: Touching a Finger to the Flame (Franklin, WI: Sheed & Ward, 2003).

2. Insights drawn from Anne Thurston, *Knowing Her Place: Gender and the Gospels* (Mahwah, NJ: Paulist Press, 1999).

3. Adapted from a prayer by Birgitta of Sweden.

4. Janet Morley, "Sing Out My Soul" in *All Desires Known*, expanded edition (Harrisburg, PA: Morehouse Publishing, 1992), 76.

5. Anselm of Canterbury, in *The Prayers and Meditations of Saint Anselm with the Proslogion*, trans. Benedicta Ward, S.L.G. (New York: Penguin Books, 1973) 153–56.

Chapter Six

1. "Act of Faith" in *Lord Hear Our Prayer*, eds. William G. Storey and Thomas McNally, C.S.C. (Notre Dame, IN: Ave Maria Press, 1978), 19.

2. "Act of Hope" in Storey and McNally, *Lord Hear Our Prayer*, 19.

3. "Act of Love" in Storey and McNally, *Lord Hear Our Prayer*, 20.

4. Alphonsus Liguori in "Living with Christ," June 2010, 13.

5. Prayer of Ignatius of Loyola.

6. "The Suscipe," in Storey and McNally, *Lord Hear Our Prayer*, 31.

Part Three: An Invitation to Pray Together

1. Andrew Greeley, *The Catholic Imagination* (Berkeley: University of California Press, 2000), 1.

Chapter Seven

1. Mark Searle in *Liturgical Gestures, Words, Objects*, ed. Eleanor Bernstein, C.S.J. (Notre Dame, IN: Notre Dame Center for Pastoral Liturgy, 1995), 9.

2. Chris Diensberg, in Bernstein, *Liturgical Gestures*, 24.

3. Marianne Murphy, in Bernstein, *Liturgical Gestures*, 28.

4. Barbara Schmich, in Bernstein, *Liturgical Gestures*, 35.

5. William G. Storey, in Bernstein, *Liturgical Gestures*, 51.

6. Estelle Martin, R.S.M., in Bernstein, *Liturgical Gestures*, 53.

7. Mark Searle in Bernstein, *Liturgical Gestures*, 53.

Chapter Eight

1. Psalm 33 in *Psalter for the Christian People*, eds. Gordon W. Lathrop and Gail Ramshaw (Collegeville, MN: The Liturgical Press, 2002), 46–47.

2. Ibid., 125–26.

3. Tich Nhat Hanh in Roberts and Amidon, *Earth Prayers*, 335.

4. J. Frank Henderson, *A Prayer Book for Remembering the Women* (Chicago: Liturgy Training Publications, 2001), 161. Used with permission.

5. Ibid., 144.

6. Dietrich Bonhoeffer, "Morning Prayer," in Nelson and Witt, *Pocket Prayers*, 70–71.

7. Ligia de Milla in Ballenger, *Prayer without Borders*, 29.

8. Ballenger, *Prayer without Borders*, 54.

9. Patrick of Ireland.

10. Henderson, *A Prayer Book*, 160.

11. Queen Mary Stuart in *Lord Hear Our Prayer, Revised Edition*, eds. William G. Storey and Thomas McNally, C.S.C. (Notre Dame, IN: Ave Maria Press, 2000), 36–37.

12. Cora Tabing-Reyes, "A Silent Moment," in Ballenger, *Prayer without Borders*, 91.

13. Thérèse of Lisieux, "My Song for Today," in Goulart, *God Has No Religion*, 232.

14. Teresa of Avila.

15. "Scottish Gaelic Song."

16. William John Fitzgerald, *A Contemporary Celtic Prayer Book* (Chicago: ACTA Publications, 1999), 40.

17. Ballenger, *Prayer without Borders*, 54.

18. Ballenger, *Prayer without Borders*, 55.

19. Rabbi Rami M. Shapiro in Roberts and Amidon, *Earth Prayers*, 371.

20. Henderson, *A Prayer Book*, 96.

21. John Henry Newman, *Heart to Heart: A Cardinal Newman Prayer Book* (Notre Dame, IN: Christian Classics, 2011), 175.

22. Marianne Williamson, *Illuminated Prayers* (Old Saybrook, CT: W.S. Konecky, 1997), 58–59.

23. Fitzgerald, *A Contemporary Celtic Prayer Book*, 42.

24. Nelson and Witt, *Pocket Prayers*, 25–26.

25. *Let There Be Light: Based on the Visionary Spirituality of Hildegard of Bingen: 30 Days with a Great Spiritual Teacher*, ed. John Kirvan (Notre Dame, IN: Ave Maria Press, 1997), 40.

26. Nelson and Witt, *Pocket Prayers*, 35.

Chapter Nine

1. Sisters of St. Joseph of Medaille, *Daily Prayer, Daily Bread: Advent*. Published privately by the Congregation.

2. Ibid.

3. Traditional Evening Hymn for Advent.

4. St. Augustine.

5. Traditional Evening Hymn for Advent.

6. William G. Storey, *A Seasonal Book of Hours* (Chicago: Liturgy Training Publications, 2001), 9.

7. Ibid., 55–56.

8. Johannes Pinsk, *Cycle of Christ: The Mass Texts Interpreted in the Spirit of the Liturgy*, trans. Arthur Gibson (New York: Desclee, 1966), 191.

9. Thomas Keating, *The Mystery of Christ: The Liturgy as Spiritual Experience*, (New York: Continuum, 1987), 13.

10. Caryll Houselander, *The Reed of God* (Notre Dame, IN: Christian Classics, 2006), 58–59.

11. John Henry Newman.

12. Pierre Teilhard de Chardin, *The Divine Milieu*, trans. Bernard Wall (NY: Harper and Row, 1960), 66.

Chapter Ten

1. Alexander Bogolepov, *Orthodox Hymns of Christmas, Holy Week and Easter* (New York: Russian Orthodox Theological Fund, 1965).

2. Ibid.

3. A. Hamman, O.F.M., *Early Christian Prayers*, trans. Walter Mitchell (Chicago: Regnery Gateway, 1961), 97.

4. Caryll Houselander, in Storey and McNally, *Lord Hear Our Prayer*, 198.

5. "Sweet Little Jesus Boy" by Robert Macgimsey.

6. "The Blessing of a Home," in *New Zealand Prayer Book*, (NY: Harper Collins, 1997), 762.

7. Caryll Houselander, *A Child in Winter: Advent, Christmas, and Epiphany with Caryll Houselander*, ed. Thomas Hoffman (Franklin, WI: Sheed & Ward, 2000), 101.

8. Keating, *The Mystery of Christ*, 16.

9. "Lo, How a Rose E'er Blooming," late sixteenth century.

10. Sidney Callahan, *The Magnificat: The Prayer of Mary*, (New York: The Seabury Press, 1975), 47–49.

11. H.A. Reinhold, *The Dynamics of Liturgy* (New York: Macmillan, 1961), 66–67.

12. Keating, *The Mystery of Christ*, 17.

Chapter Eleven

1. *Daily Prayer, Daily Bread*, Sisters of St. Joseph of Medaille, 75.

2. Adapted by the author from a Jewish Prayer.

3. Storey, *A Seasonal Book of Hours*, 140.

4. *The Summit Choir Book*, ed. Sister Maria of the Cross (New Jersey: Dominican Nuns of Summit, 1983), 481.

5. Jane Austen.

6. Ballenger, *Prayer without Borders*, 40.

7. Williamson, *Illuminated Prayers*, 80–81.

8. Keating, *The Mystery of Christ*, 37.

9. Byzantine Vespers.

10. Robert Farrar Capon, *An Offering of Uncles: The Priesthood of Adam and the Shape of the World* (New York: Harper and Row, 1967) 154.

11. Caryll Houselander, *The Letters of Caryll Houselander: Her Spiritual Legacy*, ed. Maisie Ward (New York: Sheed & Ward, 1965), 4.

Chapter Twelve

1. *Ubi Caritas*, trans. Omer Westendorf (Chicago: GIA Publications).

2. From the Taizé community. Used with permission.

3. Storey and McNally, *Lord Hear Our Prayer*, revised edition, 161–62.

4. William G. Storey, *Bless the Lord* (Notre Dame, IN: Ave Maria Press, 1980), 150.

5. Mechthild of Magdeburg, *Meditations with Mechthild of Magdeburg*, ed. Sue Woodruff (Santa Fe, NM: Bear and Company, 1982), 56.

6. From the Taizé community. Used with permission.

7. Thomas Aquinas, "Pange Lingua."

8. Venantius Fortunatus, "Pange Lingua."

9. Ancient acclamation used at the Veneration of the Cross.

10. Traditional acclamation to Christ the Savior.

11. Storey, *A Seasonal Book of Hours*, 209.

12. Gateley, *Psalms of a Laywoman*, 117.

13. William G. Storey, *Bless the Lord!* (Notre Dame, IN: Ave Maria Press, 1980), 150.

14. Storey, *A Seasonal Book of Hours*, 213.

15. "Stabat Mater," Thirteenth century traditional hymn in *Triduum Sourcebook*, 62.

16. Romano Guardini in *How Firm a Foundation: Voices of the Early Liturgical Movement*, ed. Kathleen Hughes, R.S.C.J. (Chicago: Liturgy Training Publications, 1990), 114.

17. Caryll Houselander, *The Way of the Cross*, (New York: Sheed and Ward 1955), 140–141.

18. Byzantine Daily Worship, LTP's Triduum, p. 161. From *Byzantine Daily Worship*, ©1969. Quoted with permission of Alleluia Press, Allendale, NJ.

19. Storey, *A Seasonal Book of Hours*, 274.

20. Commission Francophone Cistercienne, *La Nuit, Le Jour* (Paris: Desclee, 1973), 53.

21. Patrick Regan, "The Candle," *Easter: The Fifty Days* (Washington, DC: The Liturgical Conference), 69.

22. Keating, *The Mystery of Christ*, 187.

23. Alexander Schmemann, "Triduum," in *Great Lent: Journey to Pascha* (St. Vladimir's Seminary Press, 1974), 2.

24. Melito of Sardis, *On Pascha and Fragments*, ed. and trans. Stuart George Hall (Oxford: Clarendon Press, 1979), 90.

25. Flora Slosson Wuellner in Klug, *Soul Weaving*, 90.

26. Gerard Manley Hopkins, S.J., "The Wreck of the Deutschland," in *Poems of Gerard Manley Hopkins*, Second Edition, ed. Robert Bridges (London: Oxford University Press, 1935), 23.

27. Daniel Berrigan, S.J.

Chapter Thirteen

1. "Come Holy Spirit," in Storey and McNally, *Lord Hear Our Prayer*, 23.

2. The Sisters of Mercy, *"Morning and Evening Prayer"* (Institute of the Sisters of Mercy, 1998), 3.

3. Ibid., 3.

4. Worship Workshop, *WCC Assembly*, Melbourne, 1990.

5. Caryll Houselander in Storey and McNally, *Lord Hear Our Prayer*, 231.

6. Pope John XXIII, "To the Holy Spirit," in Storey and McNally, *Lord Hear Our Prayer*, 239.

7. Pope John XXIII in Storey and McNally, *Lord Hear Our Prayer*, 242.

8. "Veni, Sancte Spiritus," trans., John Webster Grant, in Storey and McNally, *Lord Hear Our Prayer*, 229–230.

9. Gerard Manley Hopkins, "God's Grandeur," in *The Poems of Gerard Manley Hopkins*, second ed., W. H. Gardner and N. H. MacKenzie (London: Oxford University Press, 1935), 26.

10. Balthasar Fischer, *Signs, Words and Gestures* (New York: Pueblo Publishing, 1981) 63.

11. Paul VI, "The Church's Greatest Need," in Storey and McNally, *Lord Hear Our Prayer*, 241–42.

Eleanor Bernstein, C.S.J., is a member of the Congregation of St. Joseph and holds master's degrees in theology and liturgical studies from the University of Notre Dame. She has been a high school religion teacher and a parish minister, and worked for eighteen years at the Notre Dame Center for Liturgy, for many years as its director. She served as the general editor and major contributor for a four-volume prayer book series for her Congregation. Eleanor is on the staff of the Magnificat Center in Wichita, Kansas, with a focus on adult faith formation and spirituality. She brings to her work the experience of seeking authentic prayer expression in her own life, and also the diverse prayer experiences of many others.